Carter G. Woodson

Dr. Carter Godwin Woodson, 1875-1950. Courtesy of the Association for the Study of Afro-American Life and History, Washington, D.C.

Carter G. Woodson
A Bio-Bibliography

Compiled by **SISTER ANTHONY SCALLY**

Bio-Bibliographies in Afro-American and African Studies, Number 1

G
P

Greenwood Press
Westport, Connecticut • London, England

Library of Congress Cataloging in Publication Data

Scally, M. Anthony (Mary Anthony), 1905-
    Carter G. Woodson : a bio-bibliography.

    (Bio-bibliographies in Afro-American and African
studies, ISSN 0882-7044 ; no. 1)
    Includes index.
    1. Woodson, Carter Godwin, 1875-1950—Bibliography.
I. Title. II. Series.
Z8983.4.S27   1985   [E185.97.W77] 016.973'0496073 85-10051
ISBN 0-313-24185-6 (lib. bdg. : alk. paper)

Library of Congress Catalog Card Number: 85-10051
ISBN: 0-313-24185-6
ISSN: 0882-7044

First published in 1985

Greenwood Press
A division of Congressional Information Service, Inc.
88 Post Road West
Westport, Connecticut 06881

Printed in the United States of America

The paper used in this book complies with the
Permanent Paper Standard issued by the National
Information Standards Organization (Z39.48-1984).

10 9 8 7 6 5 4 3 2 1

To
Marion Jackson Pryde
Dr. Carter G. Woodson's Cousin
With Appreciation

Contents

Preface

Anyone writing about Carter G. Woodson discovers how difficult it is to find accurate materials. This bibliography offers the results from the search for information during the past ten years. The bibliography began as an unannotated list of 735 items (including unsigned articles) used many times by patrons of the Association for the Study of Afro-American Life and History, where the writer was Librarian for five years . Her experience shows that an expanded, updated, and annotated bibliography would help to advance the cause of truth and accuracy. Most of the accounts of Dr. Woodson contain errors of fact, not of great importance, indeed, in assessing the undoubted value of his work, but annoying and puzzling to the researcher. A chronology which establishes correctly some confusing dates follows this preface.

Included. This bibliography contains over 800 entries. The twenty-two items in the list of Woodson's books include those which he edited, those of which he was joint author, and three long pamphlets which had previously appeared as articles in The Journal of Negro History, with the location of book reviews of most of his books. Signed articles and book reviews by Woodson in his periodicals, The Journal of Negro History and the Negro History Bulletin and articles about him in these periodicals comprise about 58 percent of all entries. Woodson's book reviews are sometimes long essays. Also included are articles by and about Woodson in other periodicals, books having selections from his writings or references to him, his contributions to certain newspapers, and ten relevant dissertations and theses. The appendix contains a listing of sources of unpublished manuscripts.

Although it is certain that Woodson wrote many unsigned articles and book reviews in The Journal of Negro History and the Negro History Bulletin, this work includes only those that are signed. Time and space did not allow for the present work to identify the characteristics of

his writing in unsigned articles. Nor will you find the
annual "Report of the Director" usually appearing in the
October number of each volume of The Journal of Negro
History and issued yearly as a separate pamphlet. Though
these reports provide a fund of information, the
annotations would be repetitive. Under the heading
"Notes" in The Journal of Negro History Woodson sometimes
included a listing of books and articles related to the
Negro, and sometimes correspondence or brief news items,
such as meetings and appointments. "Notes" varied in
length from half a page to several pages. Woodson
originally included obituaries under this heading but
later placed them in a "Personal" section, at which time
he expanded the other items under "Notes". "Notes" have
not been included in this bibliography except where a
specific item mentioned seemed particularly significant.
Although numerous bibliographies devoted to black history,
black writers, the black church, and folklore contain
references to Woodson's works, it seemed excessive to
include these works here.

Arrangement

Woodson's books, the articles and book reviews he
wrote for the Journal, and the articles he wrote for the
Bulletin are in chronological arrangement under separate
headings. Inclusions about him in these publications as
well as items by or about him in other books and
periodicals are in alphabetical order. Items have been
consecutively numbered throughout. The index directs the
user by item numbers to names, titles, and subjects. In
the biography of Woodson a number in brackets identifies
in the bibliography the source of a reference or quotation.
Woodson contributed extensively to newspapers, writing
more loosely and personally than in his books and magazine
articles. He often resorted to invective and railed
against persons or organizations whose actions he found
offensive, such as the segregation policies of the YMCA.
Here one finds the frank expression of his opinions. He
sometimes submitted the same articles to several papers
simultaneously (probably syndicated), or, judging by
dates, at different times. Some articles are reviews of
books and some make autobiographical references not found
elsewhere. It has not been feasible to locate and include
all the newspapers to which he contributed.
The compiler has handled and read in whole or in part
all the published articles included. The dissertations
have been located through the Dissertation Index and
Dissertation Abstracts and annotated from the abstracts,
with the exception of Dr. Patricia Romero's and Noreen
Hale's works which have been read in full. Those titles
contributed by Dr. Jacqueline Goggin appear as she gave
them.
The chief manuscript resources related to Dr. Woodson
exist in the Library of Congress, in the Moorland-Spingarn

Research Center at Howard University, and in the National Archives of the United States. But there are other smaller deposits, located chiefly through the National Union Catalog of Manuscript Collections. A listing appears in the Appendix of this volume.

The annotations are intended to be informative, not critical or evaluative, except where errors of fact are pointed out in articles about Woodson. Annotations of book reviews contain only Woodson's opinion of the book, not the compiler's.

Although "black" is the acceptable term today for a person of African ancestry, in Woodson's time the acceptable term was "Negro". Woodson used both terms as well as "colored". In an appendix to The Mis-Education of the Negro which he entitled "Much Ado About a Name" he stated that concern over such a matter was ridiculous, and said, "It does not matter so much what the thing is called as what the thing is."

Though there will, of course, be omissions here, the compiler hopes that this volume will help those persons who are interested in the work of Carter G. Woodson but have found obstacles in the way of obtaining the information they seek.

I wish to thank especially Dr. Jacqueline Goggin, who in the initial stages of this work was helpful and encouraging, Tina Raheem who typed the manuscript, Willie Leanna Miles and Dr. Marilyn Nickels who located elusive items for me, and my perceptive editor, Mary Sive, for valuable suggestions.

SAMPLE ENTRIES

Books

A book entry, whether a book by Woodson, one he reviewed, or one which includes a selection by him or discusses him, is read as follows:

2. A Century of Negro Migration. Washington, D.C.: ASNLH, 1918. Repr. Russell, 1969. (ISBN 0-8462-1319-2). AMS (ISBN 0-404-00241-2).

Explanation. This book by Woodson, A Century of Negro Migration, was published in Washington, D.C. by the Association for the Study of Negro Life and History in 1918. It was reprinted by another publisher, Russell, in 1969. The ISBN number is that publisher's order number. It was reprinted again by AMS, another publisher. There is no date to indicate when. The AMS order number is given.

Magazine Articles

16. "Some Attitudes of English Literature." 20 (1935): 27-85.

Explanation. Because this entry is in the section "Articles by Woodson in The Journal of Negro History" it indicates that an article by Woodson with the title "Some Attitudes of English Literature" can be found in Volume 20 of The Journal of Negro History, for the year 1935, on pages 27 to 85.

Abbreviations

JNH	<u>The Journal of Negro History</u>
NBH	<u>Negro History Bulletin</u>
ASNLH	The Association for the Study of Negro Life and History, now known as
ASALH	The Association for the Study of Afro-American Life and History
Dept.	Department
Diss.	Dissertation
Ed.	Editor, edited, or edition
MS	Manuscript
NAACP	National Association for the Advancement of Colored People
No.	Number
Pres.	President
Repr.	Reprint
Rev.	Revised
Ser.	Series
TS	Typescript
Trans.	Translated
Univ., Univer.	University

Chronology

1875, Dec 19	Birth, New Canton, Virginia.
1892	Left home to work on the railroad and then in the mines.
1893	Family moved to Huntington, West Virginia.
1895-1896	Attended Douglass High School, Huntington, West Virginia.
1896-1897	Attended Berea College, Kentucky.
1897, Sept-Dec	Attended Lincoln University, Pennsylvania.
1898-1900	Taught, Winona, West Virginia.
1900-1903	Principal, Douglass High School, Huntington, West Virginia.
Jun 18, 1902- Dec 1903	Attended University of Chicago.
1903	Bachelor of Literature from Berea College.
1903-1907	Taught in the Philippines.
1907	Travelled in Europe and Asia. Attended the Sorbonne, Paris.
1907, Oct-Dec	Attended University of Chicago.
1908, Jan-Aug	Attended graduate School, University of Chicago. Received B.A. in March, M.A. in August.
1908-1909	Attended Harvard University.
1909-1918	Taught, M Street (Dunbar) High School, Washington, D.C.
1912	Ph.D. in History from Harvard University.
1913 or 1914- 1921	Member of the American Negro Academy.
1915, Apr	The Education of the Negro Prior to 1861 published.

1915, Sept	Established The Association for the Study of Negro Life and History.
1917, Aug 29	First biennial meeting of ASNLH.
1918	A Century of Negro Migration published.
1918-1919	Principal, Armstrong Manual Training School, Washington, D.C.
1919-1920	Dean, School of Liberal Arts at Howard University.
1920-1922	Dean, West Virginia Collegiate Institute (West Virginia State College). Established Associated Publishers.
1921	Received grant from the Carnegie Institution. The History of the Negro Church published.
1922	The Negro in our History published.
1924	Free Negro Owners of Slaves in the U.S. in 1830: Together with Absentee Ownership of Slaves in the U.S. in 1830 published.
1925	Free Negro Heads of Families in the United States in 1830 published.
1926	Negro Orators and Their Orations published. The Mind of the Negro as Reflected in Letters Written During the Crisis, 1800-1860 published. Established Negro History Week. Received Spingarn Medal.
1927	Appointed to Advisory Committee Interracial Relations Committee on Problems and Policy Social Science Research Council. Appointed staff contributor, Dictionary of American Biography.
1928	Negro Makers of History published. African Myths: Together with Proverbs published.

1928   Attended summer meeting Social
                        Science Research Council,
                        Dartmouth College.

1929   The Negro as a Businessman, with
                        John H. Harmon Jr., and Arnett G.
                        Lindsay published.

1929-1933, 1938   Established Woodson Collection at
                        the Library of Congress.

1930   The Negro Wage Earner, with
                        Lorenzo Greene published.
                        The Rural Negro published.

1932   The encyclopedia controversy.

1932-1935   Summers in Europe.

1933   The Mis-education of the Negro
                        published.

1934   The Negro Professional Man and the
                        Community, with Special Emphasis
                        on the Physician and the Lawyer
                        published.

1935   The Story of the Negro Retold
                        published.

1936   The African Background Outlined
                        published.

1937   Began publication of the Negro
                        History Bulletin.

1939   African Heroes and Heroines
                        published.

1941   Doctor of Laws from West Virginia
                        State College.

1942   The Works of Francis J. Grimke, in
                        four volumes, published.

1950, Apr 3   Died suddenly.

1958   Elected to the Ebony Hall of Fame.

Biography

Known as "The Father of Black History," Carter G. Woodson holds an outstanding position in any consideration of the first half of the 20th century. Dr. Charles H. Wesley has said of him, paraphrasing Winston Churchill, "Never did anyone with so little bring self-respect to so many." The avowed enemy of jim crow, he devoted every waking moment of his life to fighting this foe to the finish, and he enlisted in the same struggle everyone else who would heed him. Through the two magazines which he edited and the eighteen books he wrote he reached a scholarly audience, and through the Association for the Study of Negro Life and History and Negro History Week he reached out to schools and the general public with the news that blacks had so much to be proud of in their heritage.

The period into which Carter Woodson was born was called by Dr. Rayford Logan the nadir, the lowest point, in Negro history. With the Emancipation Proclamation in 1863, a spirit of jubilee had developed among the Negro people who expected recognition as citizens who could vote and the removal of restraints to education and employment. At first when a few Negroes in the South were elected to state and federal offices it seemed that these dreams would come true. But in 1877 the Hayes-Tilden sell-out dealt a death-blow to their hopes and plunged the Negro people, recently in slavery, into a similar or worse state of peonage and terrorism. By this time the North had abandoned the blacks to their fate. Having preserved the Union and removed the competition of the cotton planters, they wanted only to return to normal pursuits.

Carter Woodson's parents, Anne Eliza (Riddle) and James Henry Woodson, were former slaves who could neither read nor write. Nevertheless, Carter Woodson credits his father with the influence which determined the course of his life. His father, he wrote in the New York Age, (6/25/32) insisted that when you learn to accept insult, to compromise on principle, to mislead your fellowman, or to betray your people, you have lost your soul. Be polite to everyone but insist always on recognition as a human being; do not do for the traducer of the race anything he will not do for you.

Anne Eliza and James Henry Woodson, when but recently married, had crossed the mountains on foot from Buckingham County, Virginia, to the new town of Huntington, West Virginia, on the Ohio River, to work on the Chesapeake and Ohio Railroad being constructed by Collis P. Huntington, for whom the town was named. Jobs were plentiful and money available, drawing there many workers from rural Virginia. However, the sanitary conditions in the raw new town were deplorable and epidemics frequent, and Anne Eliza, after losing two babies in a whooping-cough epidemic feared for the lives of her other four children. Consequently, the Woodsons in 1874 returned to the more healthful environment of rural Virginia where many of their relatives lived. There in New Canton, Buckingham County, on December 19, 1875, Carter Godwin Woodson was born. He was later joined by two little sisters, Bessie and Susie. Carter was the seventh of nine children (counting the two who died) and the youngest of four living sons.

Woodson learned about slavery first-hand from those who had experienced it. Anne Eliza, when only eleven years old, had tried to prevent the sale of her mother in order not to separate her from her small children. She begged her master to sell her instead. He placed Anne Eliza on the auction block three times, but as no one offered a sufficient amount for the little girl to pay her master's debts he resorted to selling her mother and two of her small children for $2,300.

James Henry Woodson had been hired out by his owner to dig ditches for a man named James Stratton. But James Woodson, who had learned how to build things from his father, a cabinet maker, constructed rough furniture and fish traps at night to sell for small amounts of money. This angered Stratton who went after Woodson in the ditch where he was working and attacked him with a whip. Woodson turned on his employer and thrashed him soundly instead. Then he made his way secretly toward the Union lines and served in the Union army for the remainder of the Civil War.

Many other stories of slave experiences were traditional in the Woodson and Riddle (Barnett) families.

On his return from Huntington to New Canton, Carter Woodson's father purchased a house and ten acres of land and planted tobacco. As his family grew, he added rooms to the house. Because the children had to help their father with the crop, Carter spent but very little time in the rural school taught by his two uncles, John Morton Riddle and James Buchanan Riddle. When he learned to read, his father required him to read to him every day from whatever discarded newspapers they could salvage. It was stale news, but a small window opening on a wider world. To alleviate their poverty the older sons looked toward the West where anyone could earn money building the railroad and opening the coal mines of West Virginia.

When Carter was seventeen, he joined his oldest brother Robert who had crossed the mountains some years earlier and had returned to New Canton with tales of money for the making. After helping to build the railroad in 1892, Woodson tells us, they found more lucrative employment as coal miners at Nutallburg, Fayette County. The rest of the family moved back to Huntington in 1893, one attraction being that Susie and Bessie could continue their education at the Douglass High School for Negroes which had recently opened in the town.

The family would now have consisted only of the parents and the two girls. William had previously gone to work in the mines, and after a violent altercation with Robert, had moved on to Pittsburgh; Cora had moved to Washington, D.C. with a family for whom she worked; and James had gone to Alabama.*

Woodson joked about an experience in the mines when a piece of slate fell on him and injured his head. But the experience in the mines that seemed to have impressed him most was his acquaintance with Oliver Jones. This friendship and the background of knowledge it made possible for him was influential on many aspects of his future, for Oliver Jones possessed a large collection of books, among them the latest on the Negro, such as Black Phalanx and Men of Mark, and he received many of the current newspapers. He was, however, unable to read and he engaged Carter Woodson to read to him. Woodson tells of him in "My Recollections of Veterans of the Civil War." [380] Oliver Jones had been a cook in his native Richmond before the Civil War. After his day's work in the coal mines he would throw open his home as a tearoom for the miners, selling ice cream and fruits. Woodson's compensation for reading to him was to have all the nice things he wanted to eat. A circle of friends of the "better type" of miners gathered about Jones, and distinguished blacks who came to town visited him, giving Woodson an opportunity to hear them discuss the trials and battles of blacks for freedom and equality. They often talked of the history of the race. Woodson wrote, "...my interest in penetrating the past of my people was deepened and intensified."

There the seed was planted which grew slowly year by year, invigorated by further studies and experiences, until it became a fully generated project, Woodson's infant Association, later to become the most influential instrument for spreading the truth about the proud heritage of black people.

In 1895, in his twentieth year, Woodson left the mine and enrolled at Douglass High School in Huntington. The extensive reading he had done had prepared him so well for these studies that he completed his courses in a year and a half and looked toward further studies in college. He learned from a magazine of Berea College, Kentucky, where

* Interview with Woodson's niece, Mrs. Belva Clark, in Huntington, W.Va., April 1974.

students could work to pay their expenses. This school, founded by John Fee, an abolitionist, was then coeducational and interracial. Berea College accepted his application. The Woodson family tradition is that when he took the train to cross the river into Kentucky his mother, whose favorite son he was, pulled her long hair over her face and wept bitterly. She could not bear to see him go so far away from her. Later she would get used to much longer and more distant separations.

After two-thirds of a year at Berea, Woodson spent a short time at Lincoln University, Pennsylvania, having received a scholarship. As the sophisticated atmosphere of this college was not congenial, he left at Christmas, on his way home stopping at Howard University to inquire about enrolling there; but, as Rayford Logan put it, he and the Secretary-Treasurer of Howard could not see eye to eye. [618] Consequently he accepted a position as teacher in Winona, West Virginia for two years, when in 1900 he was invited to become principal of the Douglass High School in Huntington.

When Bessie Woodson graduated from the Douglass High School in 1901 her brother Carter as principal presented her with her diploma. Woodson recalled that during his three years as principal, his father still required him to read aloud to him, and his mother required him every Sunday morning to carry breakfast to his father at the C&O RR Shops. Sunday breakfast was a special meal in the Woodson family.

Meanwhile, in 1902, Woodson matriculated at the University of Chicago, and resigned from the Douglass High School in 1903 to attend the university full time. Here a letter reached him from the Bureau of Education, Manila, dated August 31, 1903, offering him a position as teacher in the Philippine Islands, newly acquired by the United States in the Spanish-American War. As the letter was delayed in forwarding from Huntington, his acceptance was not sent until October 17.

Stories passed down from those who knew him at that time tell of his efforts to find a bride to take with him to the Philippines. He made at least three attempts, the first in Chicago where he approached the home of a young lady who, he thought, was seriously interested in him, only to see her reflection on the window blind in the embrace of another man. In Huntington, he considered proposing to a young school teacher to whom he was attracted. Again he visited without making an appointment. Finding the young woman in slovenly attire, he withdrew in haste. He could never marry anyone who looked like that! His third approach was to a young girl just out of high school and still in her teens. She declared that she could never go that far away from home.

He sailed without a bride on the S.S. _Korea_ from San Francisco on November 20, 1903, with E.O. Johnson of Indianapolis, Mr. and Mrs. Martin P. Bourne of Washington, D.C., and their eleven year old daughter, also bound for Manila. They arrived on his 28th birthday. At least

December 19, 1903, is the date on his formal appointment to the Philippine Civil Service, where he was instructed to report as soon as he arrived.

His experience in the Philippines, where the teachers used American text books and taught in the English language, affected his approach to education. Every pupil started in the first grade with Baldwin's Primer which featured the red apple (a fruit unknown in the Islands), polar bears and blizzards. In The Mis-Education of the Negro [17] he gives the example of a "real educator" who did not teach his pupils to sing "Come Shake the Apple Tree," when they had never seen an apple, but rather "Come Shake the Lomboy Tree," something they had actually often done; and who spoke to them of their own native hero, Jose Rizal, instead of Washington and Lincoln. It is important, Woodson brings out, to study the history, language, manners and customs of a people in order to approach them intelligently.

He was appointed to the town of San Isidro in the Province of Nueva Ecija, on the island of Luzon. In May, at a fiesta he was attending in the town of San Juan de Guimba, a government clerk publicly insulted him. Woodson, who would never tolerate anything reflecting on his personal dignity, immediately went to Manila, reported the incident, and asked for a transfer. In mid-June he was reassigned to the next province, Pangasinan, and appointed to be supervisor of schools in the towns of Agno and Bani. When his contract was about to expire in December 1905, he signed up for another two years and continued his work in Pangasinan. But failing health compelled him to resign as of February 5, 1907.

Leaving the Philippines, he travelled westward in order to visit Asia and Europe on the way home. In his own words: "While in the St. Settlements and India I made a special study of their school systems. Not a little of my time was spent in Palestine, Egypt, Greece and Italy. I was in Europe about six months. For one semester I was a special student of European history in the University of Paris."*

When Woodson stopped to visit his family in Huntington before returning to the University of Chicago, the black citizens of the town greeted him as a celebrity because he had been "around the world," having left by the Pacific Ocean and returned by the Atlantic. He had to regale them with accounts of his experiences and they insisted that he speak in the Baptist Church about his visit to Palestine.

Woodson received both his B.A. and his M.A. from the University of Chicago in 1908, his Bachelor's in March and his Master's in August. Enrolling at Harvard University to obtain his doctorate, he attended the lectures of professors Ephraim Emerton, Charles Gross, Roger Merriman, William Munro, and most outstanding, Edward Channing, a scientific historian who stressed original sources and

---

* Letter to Director of Education, Manila, P.I., June 19, 1908. (Record Group 350. Bureau of Insular Affairs.)

objectivity, principles Woodson later ceaselessly inculcated among his researchers. Many black historians after Woodson also studied under Channing.

In the fall of 1908 he was again corresponding with the War Department to arrange for a return to the Philippine Islands. The school year in the Philippines began in June and the War Department reinstated him as of June 1909. But Woodson wrote that he could not sail until July. "Any arrangement for my transportation in July will be satisfactory," he wrote. On June 19 he wrote: "I have not sent the medical certificates yet; for I did not care to open up the matter until I get ready to sail. I shall try to sail on July 20th or 27th." He signed his contract and the required oath and returned them to the Bureau of Insular Affairs. Almost immediately, however, he wrote again to enclose a medical certificate written by Dr. Constantine Barnett which stated that his health could not stand a return to the climate of the Philippine Islands. Late in the summer he went to Washington, D.C. where he made his home for the rest of his life.

Immediately after his arrival Woodson began to write his dissertation for Harvard, "The Disruption of Virginia," using the resources of the Library of Congress. He completed this work and received his Ph.D. in 1912. Meanwhile, since 1909, he had been teaching History, French and Spanish at M Street High School (later Dunbar), a school with a reputation for high academic standards and college-bound graduates.

He sought to meet like-minded people, joining the Epsilon Boule, Sigma Pi Phi Fraternity February 1911. Inducted at the same time were Kelly Miller of Howard University and Judge Robert H. Terrell.

After receiving his doctorate he gave his attention to the preparation of his first book for publication, The Education of the Negro Prior to 1861. [1] Even before Putnam put it on the market in the spring of 1915, he was recognized as one of the leaders among black intellectuals. In 1914 he became a member of the American Negro Academy, a selective organization for the promotion of letters, science, and art, to which entrance was controlled by the membership. Candidates had to be recommended by six enrolled members. Its purposes were to promote the publication of scholarly work and to collect the works of black authors and archival materials, as well as to "vindicate" the race from vicious assaults. The annual publication usually contained a lecture delivered by one of the members at the annual meeting. In December 1914 at the 18th Annual Meeting Woodson presented a paper, "Educating the Negro before 1860." He presented other papers through the years, in December 1916 giving "Anti-Slavery Agitation Prior to the Advent of Douglass," but none was published. Although in 1915 he established the Association for the Study of Negro Life and History, he remained active in the American Negro Academy, and many members of the Academy joined Woodson's new association while remaining active in the Academy. Alfred A. Moss,

Jr., in his book <u>The American Negro Academy</u>, [537] says that informal relations existed between the new organization and the Academy, marked by strong feelings of respect and good will on both sides. A strong attraction for Academy members was the new association's organ, <u>The Journal of Negro History</u>, to which they contributed articles. There was also the belief among some members of the Academy that Woodson's work was an extension of the Academy's. The two organizations co-existed until 1928.

The group of five who founded the Association for the Study of Negro Life and History could not then have realized how far-reaching would be the results of their meeting. Woodson was in Chicago in the late summer of 1915, using the University of Chicago Library for research. Since the completion of the YMCA Branch at 36th and Wabash Avenue he had made his headquarters there when he was in Chicago. The new Executive Secretary of this Branch, Alexander L. Jackson, permitted Woodson to use his office for meetings and discussions. On September 9, 1915, besides Dr. Woodson and Mr. Jackson, three other persons were present: George Cleveland Hall, W. B. Hartgrove, and J. E. Stamps. After an informal discussion, they formed the Association for the Study of Negro Life and History, and appointed Dr. Woodson to be the Executive Director.

Many motives impelled Woodson to take this step. Those who believed he was attempting to duplicate the American Negro Academy did not take into consideration the selective nature of Academy membership which reached only a small group of intellectuals. Woodson may have been impelled to counteract the influence of "The Birth of a Nation," then running with great acclaim in theaters all over the country. Based on Thomas Dixon's novel, <u>The Clansman</u>, the film vilified the black man and glorified the Ku Klux Klan. Dixon said in an interview that "one purpose of his play was to create a feeling of abhorrence in white people against colored men": "that he wished to have all Negroes removed from the United States and that he hoped to help in the accomplishment of that purpose by 'The Birth of a Nation'." Dr. Woodson feared that uninformed blacks (as most were then) would believe such lies as those in the film. To counteract its evil influence, his association would tell <u>all</u> <u>people</u>, black and white, the truth about the blacks' past, both their achievements in Africa and the part they had played in establishing America and in making the country great.

Other developments of the time influenced Dr. Woodson's mind in 1915, not the least of which must have been numerous restrictions of the rights of Negroes during the administrations of Taft and Wilson, and the angry confrontation of the fiery editor of the <u>Boston Guardian</u>, Monroe Trotter, and President Wilson; perhaps even his own rejection by the Harvard Club of Washington, D.C. The Harvard men of Washington had invited him to join, and he filled out an application, only to be visited by the president of the club who explained that his application could not be accepted because he was colored.*

In October 1915, less than a month after its establishment, Woodson had the new organization incorporated in Washington, D.C. Its purposes were to save and publish the records of the Negro that the race might not become a negligible factor in the thought of the world, to collect sociological and historical data, to promote studies in the field, to publish books on the Negro, and so to bring about harmony between the races through mutual understanding. By his strong assertion that black Americans were in no way inferior to white Americans, Woodson challenged head on-the then current dynamic force of Social Darwinism which justified belief that the place of blacks was unalterably on the bottom rung of the social and intellectual ladder. The survival of the fittest justified racism and made it attractive.

The following January he dropped a bomb with the publication of the first issue of The Journal of Negro History entirely without the knowledge or approval of his officers or board. They reacted with anger and indignation, though the scholarly public received the new periodical with enthusiasm.

Further recognition of Woodson as one of the significant black intellectuals came in his invitation to attend the Amenia Conference, August 24-26, 1916, as a guest of Dr. Joel E. Spingarn for three days at his home "Troutbeck." Fifty leaders representing every aspect of thought and activity gathered for frank and free discussion to establish a unity of purpose for greater progress by black Americans. [507] No reporters were allowed on the premises. Though the NAACP approved and supported the conference, that organization exercised neither authority nor responsibility over the proceedings. In a small pamphlet privately printed in 1925, W.E.B. DuBois wrote that the Conference marked the end of an era and the beginning of a new one, the end of the old way of attacking the race problem and a "Close ranks!" in facing the situation in the future.

The first two years of the Association for the Study of Negro Life and History were difficult ones, but Woodson had the support and assistance of the Secretary-Treasurer, Rev. Jesse Moorland, an officer in the YMCA and a Trustee of Howard University. Almost every day they exchanged letters about the Association's finances, Woodson's often caustic and critical, Moorland's conciliatory, sometimes with expressions of esteem for the Director. By 1917 Woodson felt secure enough to call the first meeting of the Association. Held in Washington in 1917, the group he brought together may have been the "largest number of useful and scholarly Negroes ever assembled at the national capital." Some nationally distinguished white persons also attended. [343]

The following year, after nine years at M Street High School (Dunbar), Woodson accepted the post of principal of

* Crisis: 10 (Feb. 1915): 165.

Armstrong Manual Training School. That year also his second book appeared, A Century of Negro Migration. [2] In 1919 he left Armstrong to become Dean of the College of Liberal Arts at Howard University. Arnett Lindsay, the one graduate student to persevere to the end in his class, describes him as a stern and exacting teacher, but an inspiring one who could lecture for hours without using notes. Lindsay remained a close friend of Woodson's all his life. But Dr. Woodson and the last white president of Howard University, J. S. Durkee, came to a parting of the ways in 1920. Durkee had confrontations with other faculty members also, notably Thomas Wyatt Turner, the botanist, Kelly Miller, whom he called a "contemptible puppy," and Alain Locke, the Rhodes scholar, whom he dismissed. Woodson's opinion of Durkee never changed. Invited in November 1925 to address the annual meeting of the Maryland Teachers Association with President Durkee appearing on the same program, Woodson replied to L. S. James, President of the Association: "I regret to inform you that under these circumstances I shall not serve. I would not disgrace myself by appearing on the platform with any man who has insulted and exploited the Negro Race to the extent that Durkee has." [798]

John W. Davis, the President of West Virginia Collegiate Institute (later West Virginia State College) invited him to join the faculty of that institution, convinced that he could raise its standards. Woodson took his meals at the President's house where he could also enjoy the presence of Dr. Davis's three little girls, and he took the children walking about the campus so often that people used to ask, "Whose children are those anyway?" From West Virginia he continued to direct the affairs of the Association for the Study of Negro Life and History, and while there he organized in 1921 The Associated Publishers, a company for publishing books on black subjects. When the good news reached him that the Carnegie Corporation had made him a grant of $25,000 to be paid at the rate of $5,000 a year and the Laura Spelman Rockefeller Memorial had appropriated a like sum to be paid in a similar manner, he gave up teaching in 1922 to devote his full time to the work of the Association.

Woodson sought outlets for his ideas by sending articles to black newspapers, among them Marcus Garvey's Negro World, to which he contributed historical articles for a short time after World War I. Garvey reciprocated by reviewing Woodson's books. Both Garvey and Woodson advocated black pride, but their approaches and methods differed radically. Garvey incurred the wrath of many black leaders, especially by his toleration of the Ku Klux Klan. Following Garvey's speech in New Orleans and his conference with the Acting Imperial Wizard of the KKK in Atlanta, A. Philip Randolph, a strong opponent of Garvey, received in the mail from New Orleans a human hand, accompanied by a letter from the Klan, saying Randolph had better be a paid up member of Garvey's organization within a week. In September of 1922, Chandler Owen sent a

questionnaire to twenty-five prominent Negroes, one of them Carter Woodson, for a symposium to be published in Randolph's magazine, The Messenger, as follows:
1.   Do you think Garvey's policy correct for the American Negro?
2.   Do you think Garvey should be deported as an alien creating unnecessary mischief?
3.   Remarks:
Fourteen persons replied, some at length.   Woodson's brief reply, published with the others in December 1922, said:
"Replying to your communication of September 21, I beg leave to say that I have given such little attention to the work of Marcus Garvey that I am not in a position to make an estimate of his career." [492]
Woodson then stopped sending articles to Negro World, "despite," Theodore G. Vincent reports, "pleadings from his friend William Ferris." [492]
That Woodson never married has often been observed with curiosity, both during his lifetime and since his death.   Some friends at times tried to match him up with suitable women, and interviewers teased him about imaginary romances.   He took this goodnaturedly.   One anecdote told by Woodson himself to Rayford Logan has been frequently repeated: how he entered a hotel and saw an attractive lady seated in the lobby.   Approaching her he asked, "Haven't I met you somewhere before?"   Her answer: "You certainly have.   You proposed to me once."   As a man with a cause, he was wedded only to his work and declared that no woman could stand to share his rigid regimen.   He lived in two rooms on the top floor of the Association's offices on Ninth Street, where the basement was used as a warehouse for books.   His dedication to the work of the Association absorbed him totally.   He resisted all attempts at persuasion to allow the Association to be affiliated with a college or university or any other organization and steadfastly maintained independence of operation.
From 1921 to 1930 Dr. Woodson produced eleven books: The History of the Negro Church (1921); The Negro in Our History (1922); Free Negro Owners of Slaves in the United States in 1830: Together with Absentee Ownership of Slaves in 1830 (1924); Free Negro Heads of Families in the United States in 1830 (1925); Negro Orators and their Orations (1926); The Mind of the Negro as Reflected in Letters Written During the Crisis, 1800-1860 (1926); Negro Makers of History (1928); African Myths: Together with Proverbs (1928); The Negro as a Businessman with John H. Harmon, Jr. and Arnett G. Lindsay (1929); The Negro Wage Earner with Lorenzo Greene (1930); and The Rural Negro (1930).
The Negro in Our History, [6] a textbook designed to present in succinct form a history of the United States as it has been influenced by the presence of the Negro, bore Woodson's message into classrooms in black schools and colleges nationwide.   Alain Locke said of it that it belonged to the select class of books which have brought

about a revolution of mind. Woodson constantly revised and enlarged it to keep it up to date.

But though his work was so favorably received, he wanted to reach a wider audience, especially more children and young people. To do this he inaugurated an annual celebration, Negro History Week, to be held in February in a week embracing the birthdays of both Abraham Lincoln and Frederick Douglass. The outstanding success of this venture brought him the Spingarn Medal in 1926. In supporting Woodson's nomination for the Spingarn Medal, W.E.B. DuBois stated that Woodson had performed the most striking piece of scientific work for the Negro race in the last ten years of anyone he knew. He cited the Journal, the publishing company, and Woodson's books, calling this a marvelous accomplishment.

The success of Negro History week played into the hands of the Communist Party which used it as an effective tool for Communist propaganda. Communist historians contributed accounts of the Negro's role in American history, selecting such data as they could interpret or distort to their own purposes. They attempted to take over Negro History Week. Some people thought they originated it. Without mentioning Communism by name, Woodson issued a release from his office July 29, 1931, "The Inconsistency of The Negro Radicals," [596] in which he said that Utopian dreams have never succeeded; that elements appealing to blacks to destroy the whole economic order to right social wrongs and to assist in the revolution are trying to use them as means to an end. But in an article in the New York Age (3/14/36) he wrote, "I am not a Communist myself, and with the exception of studying the principles of Marx a little...I have never paid any attention to the doctrine." The fact that Herbert Aptheker belonged to the Party in no way lessened Woodson's regard for him, and articles by Aptheker appeared in The Journal of Negro History.

But unfortunately for the Association, Dr. Woodson's unequivocal plain-speaking brought him the enmity of a white worker in the field of Negro Education, Thomas Jesse Jones. Jones was director of the educational survey of Negro schools sponsored by the Phelps-Stokes Fund. He took the well-developed Hampton Institute as his criterion and found many struggling Negro schools below standard by comparison, and thus ineligible for funds. As the Educational Director of the Phelps-Stokes Fund from 1913-1946 he controlled its money. Dr. Woodson criticized Jones for lack of judgment in his decisions and especially for blocking the efforts of agencies in Africa. For two years Jones kept the YMCA worker Max Yergan out of South Africa after his sponsors and co-workers had financed his mission there. Woodson's criticism of Jones's policies angered him, and Jones retaliated by causing foundations to withdraw their support from Woodson's Association.

This antagonism was also a significant factor in the controversy over the proposed publication of an Encyclopedia Africana. Anson Phelps Stokes called the

conference to plan the publication, and held the first
meeting November 7, 1931, with Thomas Jesse Jones among
those present. Phelps Stokes had invited neither Woodson
nor DuBois. When someone questioned their absence, the
members voted to invite them as well as Alain Locke to the
next session on January 9, 1932. Woodson explained in a
letter to Benjamin Brawley, the secretary, why he
considered it inadvisable for him to attend, and sent a
copy to each member of the conference. He said that those
who called the meeting evidently did not want his
cooperation; that several persons at the conference knew
that since 1922 the Association for the Study of Negro
Life and History had been collecting materials for such an
encyclopedia and had actually begun work on it; that there
was so much to be done for the Negro that duplication of
effort seemed unwise; and that the conference could spend
its time profitably doing something else.

DuBois, who accepted the invitation, made several
overtures to Woodson to win his cooperation, but Woodson
was adamant. In fact, Woodson's anger was boundless when
his newly appointed assistant editor, Dr. Rayford Logan,
"accepted a position to work for the rivals." [618] He
dismissed Logan, and for several years put him on his
black list. Logan, like many others who had felt
Woodson's iron hand, continued nonetheless to support him
and his work.

Woodson showed the same spirit toward Allen Johnson,
Editor of the Dictionary of American Biography, who asked
him to contribute to the work. In the New York Age
(6/18/32) he relates that he drew up a list of Negroes who
by all means should be included. Johnson accepted some
names and rejected some, then called on Woodson to write a
few sketches. Woodson soon discovered that Johnson was
assigning the sketches of the more important Negroes to
others to be written according to order. When the editor
"refused to spell Negro with a capital letter, omitted
Benjamin Banneker altogether as unworthy of any mention,
and branded John Brown as a lunatic," [469] Woodson
resigned from the staff in protest, saying he could not
afford to be associated with one who lacked historical
perspective and showed such disregard for the truth.

In 1929 Dr. Woodson placed a deposit of over 1200
valuable documents in the Manuscript Division of the
Library of Congress. The head of the Division was his
friend J. Franklin Jameson, who earlier had been
instrumental in obtaining the Carnegie grant for the
Association. One object of the Association, according to
the Constitution adopted at the 1917 meeting, was the
collecting of sociological and historical documents. Dr.
Woodson in his ten year report (1925), "Ten Years of
Collecting and Publishing the Records of the Negro," said
though "the Association had been handicapped by lack of
funds for this particular purpose, friends appreciating
the importance of the work as a rallying point for a
significant effort have given the Association a few such
documents, and others have been purchased at the expense

of the Director." [10] In annual reports from 1926-1929
he urged the donation of letters, deeds, wills, receipts
and diaries to be preserved in the Association's archives,
and reported on the increasing number given. The emphasis
backfired. People with documents decided that if they
were so valuable they had better keep them themselves.
Nevertheless, some who felt their heirs might destroy the
old family papers gave them to Dr. Woodson for
safekeeping. By 1928 Woodson had arranged for the housing
of the collection in the Library of Congress. [553] The
Social Science Research Council granted him $4000 for
"Exploratory Work in the Discovering and Collecting of
Historical Material among Negroes in the United States."
Three American historians would supervise the work:
Professor Arthur M. Schlesinger, Chairman, Professor Guy
S. Ford of the University of Minnesota, and Professor
Carlton J. H. Hayes of Columbia University. Dr. Jameson,
in a letter to Professor Schlesinger, insisted that all
students, white or colored, must have access to the papers.

In 1931 Woodson reported at length on the desirability
of collecting documents for the Library of Congress
deposit; and in 1933 he said that he had appealed to the
Social Science Research Council for a renewal of their
grant, but they pleaded lack of funds, as did other
foundations and philanthropists. Nevertheless, the entire
deposit in the Library of Congress numbered 3,140
manuscripts. The collection today contains about 5,000
items. [451]

Woodson's interest in Africa was exceptional at a time
when most blacks disdained their African ancestry and most
whites believed black Africa had no history before
colonization. Supposedly pagan and barbarous, and playing
no role in the evolution of civilization, the African
background offered whites a motive for prejudice and
blacks a motive for an inferiority complex. Changing the
popular image of Africa was crucial to improving
self-concept in American blacks. Just as George
Washington Williams had done in his pioneer scholarly
study, History of the Negro Race in America (New York,
1882, 2 vols.), Woodson in The Negro in Our History [6]
traced blacks from their origin in Africa, presenting
Africa as a complexity of cultures, a place of the early
great empires of Ghana, Mali, Songhay; of peoples who
through cross fertilization in the Nile Valley had perhaps
given the idea of one Creator God to the Jews; then by the
fusion of peoples had contributed to the civilization of
the ancient Mediterranean region. Woodson was encouraged
by the discoveries of the anthropologist Franz Boas who at
this time was also presenting a new evaluation of Africa,
and by the work of Melville Herskovits, many of whose
ideas also paralleled his. In his studies Woodson kept
close ties with African intellectuals. He deplored the
"economic imperialism" of European countries in Africa,
particularly England, and predicted that the necessity of
modernizing the African colonies and training scholars
would produce leaders who would break the European

stranglehold and release the people from European domination before the end of the 20th century.

Woodson found in Africa in diaspora, including Afro-Americans, traces of African lineage which their forebears brought from Africa. The surviving cultural elements were mainly spiritual ones, especially an emotional nature which found its outlet in music, art and oratory.

Dr. Woodson spent the summers from 1932 to 1936 in Europe, exploring libraries for materials on Africa and making contacts to aid in his research. He reported on these trips in The Journal of Negro History and described his aims as making a survey to discover the attitudes of the Europeans toward the African and their interest in studying about Africa, the locating of documentary materials on Africa, the assigning of investigators to certain tasks, and cooperating with certain Europeans engaged in scientific study of the African. He purchased works on Africa for the Association's library while abroad. The "body of facts and observations he obtained enriched the work entitled the African Background Outlined, or Handbook for the Study of the Negro." [20] He collected data for the completion of the Encyclopedia Africana. He wrote about his European experiences at much greater length in newspaper articles than in his magazines, mentioning in the New York Age, for example, that in 1932 he became acquainted with the Countess of Jumilhav whose book of travel in Abyssinia, entitled Ethiopie Moderne, he found very interesting.

He deplored blacks who went to Europe from the United States with nothing to contribute but greased hair and loud clothes and an interest in jazz. Many of these asked him for money when they met him on the street. They could get jobs if they wished, he said, for American corporations, unwilling to employ blacks in the United States, were often willing to do so abroad. He mentioned also in his accounts of Europe that Hitler was instituting racial persecution in Germany.

Langston Hughes, Joel A. Rogers, and Charles H. Thompson, the Editor of the Journal of Negro Education, have written of meeting with Dr. Woodson abroad. Dr. and Mrs. Thompson encountered him unexpectedly in the Place de la Concorde, Paris. Woodson invited them to dinner. He took his guests to an exclusive restaurant where they were served an elaborate gourmet meal. This story gave rise to the persuasion among many that while abroad Dr. Woodson always ate gourmet meals and only in the best restaurants.

Between 1933 and 1939 Dr. Woodson produced several works. The Mis-Education of the Negro (1933) aroused controversy, although Woodson had been progagating the ideas contained in the book for several years in his lectures and newspaper articles. His main point was that the conventional public schools developed inferiority complexes in black children who should be taught to be proud of their black heritage. To overcome this complex Woodson was devoting his strength, energy, and intellect.

This was his reason for Negro History Week and for the books he wrote to be used in the schools, such as The Story of the Negro Retold (1935) and African Heroes and Heroines (1939). This period also saw The Negro Professional Man and the Community, with Special Emphasis on the Physician and the Lawyer (1934), and The African Background Outlined (1936).

His concern for school children and the requests of several teachers led him to undertake the publication of a periodical for them, less scholarly than the Journal of Negro History, appearing each month during the school year from October until June. From Woodson's description of the proposed magazine, one would never recognize the current Negro History Bulletin which has changed drastically with the different directors at the Association's offices. Woodson proposed a periodical in simplified language on the level of the child in the fifth grade to popularize black history lower down in the elementary school. Following the calendar of "Important Events and Dates in Negro History" each issue would carry a feature story, the first of which would be on slavery, followed by the free black, friends of the black in slavery, the struggle for freedom, emancipation, the beginnings of freedom, recent achievement, present status, and connections of blacks with members of the race abroad. He would also include sketches of blacks and friends of the race, historical news, activities in the schools, book reviews, questions and answers, and productions by children themselves. The Bulletin, which first appeared October 1937, did not maintain this plan for long. In 1940, the year of the 15th Negro History Week, Woodson discontinued his article on this celebration in the Journal of Negro History and reported instead in the March number of the Negro History Bulletin, but continued to include mention of Negro History Week in his Annual Report. In three years the Bulletin grew from the originally planned eight pages to twenty-four, and the contents changed to include art, literature and other achievements. In 1941 the plan was to treat blacks regionally in the United States throughout the year.

On his trip abroad in 1935, Dr. Woodson noted the rising international disturbances in Europe. As they increased in intensity in the next few years he continued to be hopeful, referring once to "when the international muddle finally clears up." That he could not go abroad to pursue his investigations in the archives of Europe seemed at first an inconvenience. In fact, the war made greater demands on the resources of the Association by increased requests from soldiers abroad for information. The United States purchased books from the Association for camp libraries and subscriptions to the Negro History Bulletin, and USO clubs celebrated Negro History Week. But in his 1943-1944 Annual Report Woodson remarked that research during the war had been greatly handicapped, there was an acute shortage of workers, and a much reduced staff, and the Association could not compete with the high salaries

offered by the Government.

He tried to see the bright side of things. Because of
the stringent travel restrictions at home, those planning
programs and celebrations for Negro History Week had to
discover   local talent for speaking engagements, which
often proved to be an advantage. And as to research, many
of those abroad sent him accounts of interesting facts and
discoveries, such as Harold Courlander's article on games
in   Abyssinia.   Meanwhile Woodson made an effort to
"exploit the few untouched sources" on Africa "on this
side of the Atlantic" which would enable him to again give
all his attention to the foreign field when the war ended.

During this time he concentrated also on simplifying
and adapting materials for children, working, for example,
with Beatrice Jackson Fleming and her sister Marion
Jackson Pryde (whose mother was his first cousin) on the
book Distinguished Negroes Abroad (1946).   Shortage of
staff and materials during the war also hampered his work
on the Encyclopedia Africana to which he called attention
in several instances in his last ten years.   In the
1939-1940 Annual Report he mentioned that he had been
studying "the careers of individuals deemed worthy to be
recorded in a dictionary of Negro biography," but decided
to combine these more than a hundred sketches with the
data already collected for the projected Encyclopedia
Africana which he proposed to publish in six volumes
within the next three years, if the paper shortage would
allow it. If this plan had worked out, the set would have
been published by 1947, but he reported then that he was
putting it into literary form and hoped to issue the first
three volumes by 1948.   He had appointed an editorial
board and had held a meeting on January 9, 1949, of
"fifteen scholars of literary standing." Unfortunately,
because of his untimely death, April 3, 1950, the
encyclopedia progressed no further than that.

Between 1941 and 1950 Dr. Woodson wrote 56 articles
for the Negro History Bulletin while for the Journal of
Negro History, except for 206 book reviews, he wrote only
three articles.   In addition he prepared "Notes" and
included his Annual Report for each volume. The book
reviews are widely diverse in scope and language, from
Three Generations, an autobiography by Charles W. Cansler
and The Big Sea by Langston Hughes, to a collection of
significant pamphlets from South Africa, to Panorama de la
Musica Afroamericana from Buenos Aires, the Annuario
Estatistico do Brasil, from Rio de Janeiro, and Afrique
Occidentale Francais from Paris. The only books he
produced at this time were the four volumes he edited in
1942 of The Works of Francis J. Grimke, his friend who
died in 1937 leaving funds for their publication and
specifying Dr. Woodson as editor.

The children on Ninth Street still begged him for
stories when he left his office; the girls at the YWCA in
whose cafeteria he often ate, still welcomed him warmly as
a friend; he still celebrated holidays with his Jackson
cousins in Washington, and still received with affection

visits from his niece Belva Bickley, Bessie's daughter; but his colleagues noticed changes in him. He was more genial in dealing with them, spoke less at meetings, and listened more to others. And he looked tired. No one expected that on April 3, 1950, he would alarm his secretary by failing to be in his office when she arrived. He had died quietly and unexpectedly during the night, alone in his Spartan apartment above his office. He was 74 years of age. His funeral was held at the Shiloh Baptist Church and he was buried in Lincoln Memorial Cemetery, Suitland, Maryland.

In his later years he saw some results of his dedicated efforts to obtain recognition for blacks. Dr. Logan points out that in 1944, realizing the need for revision of teaching materials in establishing and maintaining world peace, the American Council on Education called for a correction of inaccurate statements and omissions in texts dealing with our international neighbors. [351] UNESCO also initiated studies to destroy prejudice at home and abroad. These developments were only two of many based upon Dr. Woodson's pioneering work which occurred during his lifetime. The demand for black studies in colleges and universities in the 1960's owed its impetus to his unremitting and zealous emphasis upon the importance of spreading the truth about the African and Afro-American background, and the use in elementary and high schools all over the country of his black history texts. Negro History Week developed into Black History Month in 1976 and is more widely celebrated than ever before, though few of those who take part in the celebration even know that Dr. Woodson started it. Scholar, historian, humanitarian, by his dedicated and unswerving labors, he gave the world a new picture of a glorious African past, and to a people of the diaspora, pride in their inheritance.

1.
Books by Woodson

1. The Education of the Negro Prior to 1861: A History of the Education of the Colored People of the United States from the Beginning of Slavery to the Civil War. New York: Putnam's, 1915. Repr. Ayer Co., 1968. (ISBN 0-405-01846-0)

A history of education before the Civil War which falls into two periods with 1835 as the date of division. Before this date many slaves were given schooling on the plantation; but later slavery became an industrial rather than a patriarchal institution, and slave owners considered that education would lead to too much self-assertion.

Book Review Digest (Aug. 1915)
Bookseller, New York City (1 Aug. 1915) Mistakenly attributed to George Godwin Woodson
Chesterton, Cecil "Dixie and the Wrong Turning." The New Witness [London] (16 Sept. 1915), 470-71
Cleveland Open Shelf (Aug. 1915), 75
Congregationalist, Boston, Mass. (15 July 1915)
The Crisis 10 (Sept. 1915), 251
F(leming), W(alter) L. Mississippi Valley Historical Review 2 (1916), 586-88
Gould, Joseph F. Survey 35 (29 Jan. 1916), 521-22
Independent, New York (23 Aug. 1915)
Jernegan, Marcus W. American Historical Review 21 (Apr. 1916), 634-35
The New Statesman (16 Oct. 1915)
New York Times (18 July 1915), 259
Park, Robert E. American Journal of Sociology 21 (July 1915), 119-20
Review of Reviews 52 (Sept. 1915), 379
Springfield Republican (15 Nov. 1915), 13
T.F.M. America (19 June 1915)
Terrell, Mary Church JNH 1 (1916), 96-97
Unity, Chicago, vol. xxxvi, (9 Sept. 1915), 25-27

2.   A Century of Negro Migration. Washington, D.C.:
ASNLH, 1918. Repr. Russell, 1969. (ISBN 0-8462-1319-2).
AMS (ISBN 0-404-00241-2).

The book reviews the movements of Negroes from South
to North, and other movements such as to the West
after the Civil War, and explains why Negroes
migrated, where they went, and what they have
accomplished.

American Review of Reviews 58 (Dec. 1918), 661
Boston Transcript (31 Dec. 1918), 6
Nation 108 (11 Jan. 1919), 59
Scroggs, William O. American Historical Review 24
(Apr. 1919), 520
Times Literary Supplement [London] (24 Oct. 1918), 504
Wesley, Charles H. JNH 4 (1919) 341-42.

3. The History of the Negro Church. Washington, D.C.:
Associated Publishers, 1921.

This work shows that the history of the Negro church
in America is closely related to the Negro's strivings
in all aspects of life, with his ambitions, endeavors,
songs, edifices, in all situations and circumstances.

DuBois, W.E.B. The Freeman 6 (4 Oct. 1922), 92-93
L.F. Southern Workman 51 (1922), 248
Sumner, F.C. JNH 7 (1922), 223-24

4. Fifty Years of Negro Citizenship as Qualified by the
United States Supreme Court. Repr. from JNH 6 (1921).

An objective study of the constitutional history of
the United States as it affected the freedmen in the
period under question.

5.   Early Negro Education in West Virginia. Institute, W.
Va. West Virginia State College, 1921. Published as "West
Virginia Collegiate Institute Bulletin," Series 6, No. 3.

A study bearing on the early efforts of workers among
the Negroes of West Virginia. Salient facts of the
early history of pioneer education were obtained from
a questionnaire and prepared by a committee at the
suggestion of President John W. Davis. Dr. Woodson as
chairman was given the task of organizing the report.
It contains eight brief references to Woodson or his
relatives involved in education. Also published as an
article in JNH.

6.   The Negro in Our History. Washington, D.C.:
Associated Publishers, 1922.

A textbook which went through nineteen editions during
Woodson's lifetime, the work was in its fourth edition

by 1927. Until his death, it was constantly revised
and enlarged to keep it up to date. Alain Locke said
of this book, "It belongs to that select class of
books that have brought about a revolution of mind."

American Political Science Review 16 (Nov. 1922), 727
Booklist 19 (Jan. 1923), 110
Dowd, Jerome. American Historical Review 33 (1927), 192
DuBois, W.E.B. Crisis 35 (Jan. 1928)
Harrison, Hubert. New York Tribune (7 Jan. 1923), 18
Lewinson, Paul. Mississippi Valley Historical Review
29 (June 1942), 130-31
Locke, Alain. JNH 12 (1927), 99-101
Maloney, C. McDonald. Opportunity 1 (May 1923), 27-28
Pittsburgh Monthly Bulletin 27 (Dec. 1922), 540
Springfield Republican (15 July 1922), 8
Subscription Books Bulletin 3 (Apr. 1932), 24
Survey 49 (15 Oct. 1922), 119
Tynes, Harcourt A. Opportunity 19 (Sept. 1941), 282-83
W.H.S. Southern Workman 51 (1922), 490-92

7. Free Negro Owners of Slaves in the United States in
1830: Together with Absentee Ownership of Slaves in the
United States in 1830, ed. Washington, D.C.: ASNLH, 1924.
Repr. Negro Univ. Press. (ISBN 0-8371-0761-X)

Largely a statistical compilation, this brief work was
composed chiefly from the data of the census reports
for 1820. Woodson's aim was "to promote the further
study of a neglected aspect of our history."

Crisis 31 (Feb. 1926), 191-93

8. Free Negro Heads of Families in the United States in
1830: Together with a Brief Treatment of the Free Negro.
Washington, D.C.: ASNLH, 1925.

An introduction gives pertinent facts related to the
statistics which follow. A number of Negroes were
slave-owners, in some cases controlling large
plantations. The date 1830 was selected because by
then free Negroes had reached their highest mark as a
distinct class. Having in some cases economic
interests in common with the whites, the Negro heads
of families when slave holders often enjoyed the same
social standing. Statistics are arranged by states.
An alphabetical index of names is given.

Crisis 31 (Feb. 1926), 191-93.

9. Negro Orators and their Orations, ed. Washington,
D.C.: Associated Publishers, 1926. Repr. Russell, 1969.
(ISBN 0-8462-1316-8)

This work of source readings, published as a companion
volume to The Mind of the Negro Reflected in Letters

presents "practically all of the important speeches of Negroes in print." A discussion of oratory from the point of view of the world's great thinkers compares its importance in the ancient world with its comparative unimportance today. Biographical sketches of the speakers, together with the exposition of their thoughts in the orations included, constitute a brief history of blacks in America.

Crisis 31 (Feb. 1926), 191-93
JNH 10 (Oct. 1925), 779-80
Saturday Review of Literature (9 Jan. 1926), 484

10. Ten Years of Collecting and Publishing the Records of the Negro. Washington, D.C.: ASNLH, [1926].

A short historical account of the founding of the Association for the Study of Negro Life and History and its development during the first ten years, recounting how it met its declared goals. Included are a brief financial statement, a list of the Association's strongest financial supporters, and a description of works produced through research during that time.

11. The Mind of the Negro as Reflected in Letters Written During the Crisis, 1800-1860, ed. Washington, D.C.: ASNLH, 1926. Repr. Russell, 1969 (ISBN 0-8462-1314-1) and Greenwood (ISBN 0-8371-1129-X).

This volume gives insight into the mind of the Negro during the period of slavery and is a mine of information on those times. Letters of the first section are to the American Colonization Society relating to emigration to Liberia; those of the second section deal with the anti-slavery movement, and two short concluding sections contain miscellaneous correspondence, some of it personal.

B.L. Survey 56 (15 Sept. 1926), 643
Crisis 34 (Mar. 1927), 20, 32
Johnson, Charles S. N.Y. Herald Tribune (26 Dec.1926),5
Mulherin, William A. Catholic World 124 (Dec. 1926), 427
New York Times (24 Oct. 1926), 26

12. Negro Makers of History. Washington, D.C.: Associated Publishers, 1928.

An adaptation of The Negro in Our History for elementary schools. The author has simplified the language and condensed the treatment. Each chapter is followed by "Facts to be Kept in Mind" and "Hints and Questions."

Bryant, Alice G. Southern Workman 59 (Feb. 1930), 94
Crisis 36 (Feb. 1929), 48
Davis, John. Opportunity 8 (Apr. 1930), 121

13. African Myths Together with Proverbs: A Supplementary Reader Composed of Folk Tales from Various Parts of Africa. Adapted to use of children in the public schools. Washington, D.C.: Associated Publishers, 1928.

Woodson considered folk tales of a people a guide to understanding their past. This book contains traditional legends passed on by African story tellers showing humor, moral teachings, wit, and wisdom.

B[ryant], A[lice] G. Southern Workman 59 (Jan. 1930), 48
Crisis 36 (Feb. 1929), 48

14. The Negro as Businessman, joint author with John H. Harmon, Jr. and Arnett G. Lindsay. Washington, D.C.: Associated Publishers, 1929.

Part I "As a local businessman," by J.H. Harmon; II "In Banking," by A.G. Lindsay; and III "Insurance," by C.G. Woodson. The preface is also by Woodson. The study touches on history from ante-bellum times to 1920, naming successful men and women in all three areas.

Crisis 36 (Dec. 1929), 414

15. The Negro Wage Earner, joint author with Lorenzo J. Greene. Washington, D.C.: ASNLH, 1930. Repr. AMS Press (ISBN 0-404-00163-7), Russell (ISBN 0-8462-1321-4).

This work is the first product of the three-year survey of social and economic conditions of U.S. Negroes, and shows the various occupations in which blacks have been employed, determining whether or not they have increased or decreased their numbers in these occupations.

DuBois, W.E.B. Nation 32 (8 Apr. 1931), 385-86
JNH 16 (1931), 341-42
Reid, Ira de A. Opportunity 9 (Nov. 1930), 88

16. The Rural Negro. Washington, D.C.: ASNLH, 1930. Repr. Russell, 1969 (ISBN 0-8462-1324-9).

A treatment of the conditions of health, farming, tenancy, peonage, industry, trade, religion, education and recreation of the rural South, composed largely from facts in the U.S. Census Reports and questionnaires which were sent to rural families.

Boston Transcript (16 Aug. 1930), 3

Browning, James. <u>JNH</u> 16 (1931), 245-46
<u>Crisis</u> 37 (Sept. 1930), 13, 321
Dabney, Thomas L. <u>Southern Workman</u> 59 (Oct. 1930), 477-79
<u>Herald-Tribune Books</u> (23 Nov. 1930), 14
Hill, T. Arnold. <u>Opportunity</u> 8 (Nov. 1930), 344
<u>New York Times</u> (14 Sept. 1930), 16

17. <u>The Mis-Education of the Negro</u>. Washington, D.C.: Associated Publishers, 1933. Repr. AMS Press (ISBN 0-404-16027-1).

After an exposure of educational methods by which the Negro has been plunged deeper into a consciousness of inferiority, the author proposes a definite system under which members of the race will come to a full development of their own gifts and personalities. The test which should be applied to any method of education is its power to equip people to meet the world satisfactorily. Corrective methods and suggestions are offered for a new program in the black man's education.

"Additional Notices of the Mis-Education of the Negro." <u>JNH</u> 18 (1933), 341-50
Barney, Virginia. <u>North American Review</u> 16 (Apr. 1933, 235
Bond, Horace Mann. "Dr. Woodson Goes Wool-Gathering." <u>JNH</u> 18 (1933), 222-24.
<u>Commonweal</u> 18 (12 May 1933), 55
Locke, Alain. "Black Zionism." <u>Survey</u> 69 (Oct. 1933), 363-64
<u>New York Times</u> (26 Feb. 1933), 15
"Some Notices of the Mis-Education of the Negro." <u>JNH</u> 8 (1933), 222-24.

18. <u>The Negro Professional Man and the Community: With Special Emphasis on the Physician and the Lawyer</u>. Washington, D.C. ASNLH, 1934. Repr. Negro Univ. Press (ISBN 0-8371-1896-4), Johnson Reprints (ISBN 0-384-69208-7).

The survey on which this volume was based covered almost the whole of the South and most of the large cities, with considerable coverage of populations outside the South. There is an abundance of statistical material. Although emphasis is on the medical and legal professions, Woodson does not wholly ignore other professions.

Gordon, A.H. <u>JNH</u> 20 (1935), 480-81
<u>Harvard Law Review</u> 47 (May 1934), 1303
Locke, Alain. <u>Survey</u> 70 (Aug. 1934), 267-68
Reid, Ira de A. <u>Opportunity</u> 12 (May 1934), 154
Sumner, F.C. "The Negro in the Professions." <u>Journal of Negro Education</u> 4 (1935), 113

19. <u>The Story of the Negro Retold</u>. Washington, D.C.: Associated Publishers, 1935.

An objective treatment of the history, achievements, handicaps and defects of the Negro, demonstrating his contributions to the economic development of the country, as well as to poetry and music. To be used as a semester's work in high school, the text is furnished with review questions and bibliography.

<u>Booklist</u> 32 (Apr. 1936), 236
<u>Christian Century</u> 53 (17 June 1936), 874
Clemens, Cyril <u>Commonweal</u> 24 (22 May 1936), 111
Preston, E. Delorus, Jr. <u>JNH</u> 21 (1936), 76-78
Southall, E.P. <u>Opportunity</u> 14 (Apr. 1936), 122
<u>Survey Graphic</u> 25 (Apr. 1936), 261
Wilkerson, D.A. "A High School Text for Negro History." <u>Journal of Negro Education</u> 5 (Oct. 1936), 626-29

20. <u>The African Background Outlined</u>. Washington, D.C.: ASNLH, 1936. Repr. Negro Univ. Press (ISBN 0-8371-0760-1).

A compilation of African life, culture and history, supplemented by a topical study outline with selected references for the study of American Negro life and history.

<u>Foreign Affairs</u> 15 (Oct. 1936), 216
Gallagher, B.G. <u>Christian Century</u> 53 (10 June 1936), 842
Knox, Ellis O. "A Study Guide of the Negro." <u>Journal of Negro Education</u> 5 (1936), 638-41
Logan, Rayford W. <u>JNH</u> 21 (1936), 322-24
Murphy, George G., Jr. "Woodson's Book Out." <u>Afro-American</u> (25 Apr. 1936)
<u>Survey</u> 72 (Aug. 1936), 256

21. <u>African Heroes and Heroines</u>. Washington, D.C.: Associated Publishers, 1939.

A biographical account of various Africans who rose to prominence intended for junior and senior high school students. The book stresses especially the militant resistance of the African nations and tribes to both Arabic and European invaders. Also included are a brief survey of the geography and peoples of Africa and the black states which existed there.

<u>Boston Transcript</u> (22 July 1939), 3
Lofton, Williston H. <u>JNH</u> 24 (1939), 477-78

22. <u>The Works of Francis J. Grimké</u>, ed. Vol. 1; <u>Addresses Mainly Personal and Racial</u>. Vol. 2: <u>Special Sermons</u>. Vol 3: <u>Stray Thoughts and Meditations</u>. Vol. 4: <u>Letters</u>. Washington, D.C.: Associated Publishers, 1942.

The volumes cover comprehensively the period from 1875-1935, touching all aspects of black social history. Partial biographical sketches of Dr. Grimké appear in the introduction to the first three volumes. Volume 1 consists of obituaries and biographical tributes to distinguished persons with historical references to their achievements. Included are analyses of forces obstructing racial freedom and miscellaneous addresses. In Volume 2 his sermons "reflect research in the vast laboratories of life." Volume 3 records his impressions, written from time to time as a sort of diary, begun in 1914 when his wife, Charlotte Forten Grimké, died. Volume 4 contains his extensive correspondence with black notables of his day.

Brewer, William M. JNH 27 (1942), 454-60
Mays, Benjamin E. "Works of Francis J. Grimké." Journal of Negro Education 12 (1943), 661-62.

2.
The Journal of Negro History

23. "The Negroes of Cincinnati Prior to the Civil War." 1 (1916): 1-22.

Discrimination toward Negroes in Cincinnati grew from toleration toward the early immigrants to legal proscription and open persecution. Negroes had to contend with ever stricter Black Laws in social and labor situations. As abolition societies arose schools and churches increased in number, adults and children received some education, and economic conditions improved, though prejudice continued.

24. "Freedom and Slavery in Appalachian America." 1 (1916): 132-50.

Settlers in the Appalachian region mistrusted the conservative slave-holding plantation owners, but the invention of the cotton-gin changed the attitude of many uplanders and abolition societies declined. However, the radical element continued to oppose slavery and, at the outbreak of the Civil War, forty-eight counties loyal to the Union formed the state of West Virginia.

25. "Anthony Benezet." 2 (1917): 37-50.

This eighteenth century Quaker, a Huguenot refugee and anti-slavery activist, established a "female seminary" for daughters of the aristocratic families of Philadelphia, but was especially effective in his writings about the "iniquitous practice" of slavery. In 1750, in order to establish a school for Negroes, he had to give up his school for girls.

26. "The Beginnings of the Miscegenation of the Whites and Blacks." 3 (1918): 335-53.

Peoples from Egypt and the Barbary States intermingled
with blacks from Africa in early ages and moved into
Europe leaving traces in all Mediterranean countries.
Brazil inherited a Moorish element from Portugal and
made no distinction of the races in society or
politics. But in the English Colonies stringent laws
against miscegenation could not prevent it. The
article itemizes such laws from 1661 through 1780.

27. "Negro Life and History in Our Schools." 4 (1919):
273-80.

Though historians studying the causes of the Civil War
concluded that the enslavement of Negroes was a
disgrace of which the country should feel ashamed,
southerners who went North to study tended to
vindicate slavery. Woodson lists the historians of
each period and tells where their sympathies lay. He
also tells which colleges introduced courses on Negro
history, and describes the University Commission on
Southern Race Relations.

28. "The Relations of Negroes and Indians in
Massachusetts." 5 (1920): 45-57.

In the seventeenth century many Negroes escaped to
live among the Indians. Indians who married whites
passed into the white community while those who
married Negroes passed into the black community.
Indians were subjected to hated discriminatory
guardianship laws. In 1861 the state provided Indians
citizenship and by 1869 most were citizens. The state
granted pensions to those dispossessed of land which
some Negro-Indians were still receiving in 1920. Paul
Cuffee came from the Dartmouth tribe.

29. "Early Negro Education in West Virginia." 7 (1922):
23-63

Previously published as a pamphlet by the West
Virginia Collegiate Institute this study was later
published in the JNH. It contains eight references to
Woodson or his relatives who were involved in
education.

30. "Ten Years of Collecting and Publishing the Records
of the Negro." 10 (1925): 598-606.

For annotation see no. 10.

31. "Negro History Week." 11 (1926): 238-42; 12 (1927):
103-109; 13 (1928): 121-25; 14 (1929): 109-15; 15 (1930):
125-33; 16 (1931): 125-31; 17 (1932): 119-23; 18 (1933):
107-13; 19 (1934): 111-17; 20 (1935): 123-30; 21 (1936):
105-10; 22 (1937): 141-47; 23 (1938): 139-43; 24 (1939):
137-42.

From 1926 until 1939 Woodson wrote an article on Negro History Week for the April number of <u>JNH</u>. After 1940 he included the report in "Annual Report of the Director" in the October issue. A progression can be seen in the programs from year to year.

32. "History Made to Order." 12 (1927): 330-48.

Commenting that Mr. G.E. Eaton was of apparently good intentions, Woodson in a long open letter indicates the errors in his article regarding slavery and the black church, and includes a list of readings. A letter by Lillie Buffum Chase Syman questions Eaton's veracity, and one from Woodson to Miss Carrie J. Gleed shows how she has been misled. Two more letters dealing with historical facts follow.

33. "Insurance Business Among Negroes." 14 (1929): 202-26.

After Emancipation blacks developed secret fraternal benevolent societies to take care of the sick and to bury the dead. As these projects expanded they became business enterprises leading to experience in administration and increased employment. The successful insurance companies owned and managed by blacks developed from these early fraternal orders.

34. "The Negro Washerwoman, a Vanishing Figure." 15 (1930): 269-77.

The Negro washerwoman was often the sole bread-winner of the family. In slavery she often purchased the freedom of her husband and children; in freedom she took the initiative of buying a house and educating the children, or accumulating capital to start a business. The first dimes and nickels with which some enterprises were launched came largely from these women.

35. "Notes: The Director Speaks." 16 (1931): 344-48.

Excerpts from Dr. Woodson's speeches and commencement addresses throughout the country. The schools have handicapped Negroes by teaching them that they are inferior. Negroes should appreciate their differentness and discover that particular thing which one race can do better than any other. Nothing is to be gained by mere imitation.

36. "Communications: The George Washington Bicentennial." 17 (1932): 103-106.

An open letter replying to inquiries asking how blacks should celebrate the George Washington Bicentennial. The Commission asked blacks to register to take the part of slaves in a dramatization. To dramatize Negroes only as bondsmen would be a tragic error which would not ring true to history. Woodson offered to produce a plan to emphasize commendable things about Negroes but it was rejected by the Commission.

37. "Emma Frances Grayson Merritt." 18 (1933): 351-54.

The contribution of this outstanding educator to the public schools of Washington, D.C. was unmatched. In addition to her teaching, lectures, institutes, and summer school work, she was president of the Washington Branch of the NAACP. After retirement she devoted much time to the Phillis Wheatley YWCA. Her death was a great loss to the ASNLH.

38. "Some Attitudes of English Literature." 20 (1935): 27-85.

The conditions of slaves in ancient Greece and Rome differed from slavery as commerce in the sixteenth and later centuries. English writings mention the Negro extensively in legend, drama, poetry and prose. Woodson analyzes works and characters. He summarizes novels beginning with some early obscure ones and proceeding through the twentieth century to G.B. Shaw's The Adventures of the Black Girl in Her Search for God.

39. "Attitudes of the Iberian Peninsula." 20 (1935): 190-243.

Part I distinguishes between Moors and Negroes among migrants to and from Spain and Portugal. About 1300 when King Henry and other explorers brought about expansion, Negroes could work their way to the highest levels of society. Thus Spain and Latin America escaped racial discrimination. Part II traces the mention of Negroes by Spanish writers with particular attention to Juan Latino.

40. "Notes: Dr. Melville J. Herskovits's Method Examined." 22 (1937): 293-98.

Woodson, departing from his practice of ignoring reviewers' remarks, answers Melville Herskovits' review of African Background Outlined, which charged him with anti-white prejudice, objected to the classification of Pushkin as a Negro, and questioned his objectivity. Woodson countered that an anthropologist should not review a work of history, and that Herskovits accused him of omitting material which he had included.

41. "Personal: John Franklin Jameson." 23 (1938): 131-33.

The obituary pays tribute to Woodson's friend, former

head of the Bureau of Historical Research of the Carnegie Institution of Washington, D.C., and expresses appreciation for the grant of $25,000 he obtained for ASNLH in 1921. Jameson also made valuable contributions to historical literature and was a strong promoter of black history.

42. "An Accounting for Twenty-Five Years." 25 (1940): 422-31.

Referring to previous ineffective attempts to popularize Negro history, Woodson relates the founding of the Association, lists its supporters, projects, researchers, difficulties during the depression and successful outcome. He gives a financial report. The MS. collection in the Library of Congress, Negro History Week, and publication of the Negro History Bulletin are among the achievements mentioned.

43. "Notes on the Bakongo." 30 (1945): 421-31.

The Bakongo, an admixture of tribes, are chiefly Bantu. Agricultural, but also noted for metal and woodwork, they fought among themselves before coming under European influence which developed in the usual imperialistic fashion, and created most of the Belgian Congo and Portuguese Southwest Africa. Includes an account of the Christian Queen Anna Nzinga Nbandi Ngola.

44. "Personal: Thomas Jesse Jones." 35 (1950): 107-109.

After some experience in research on the Negro, Jones became Educational Director of the Phelps-Stokes Fund (1913-1946). Woodson accused him of conducting a campaign against ASNLH and cutting off all aid from boards and foundations. Nevertheless, Woodson gave him credit for establishing Achimoto College in Africa.

45. "The Sixtieth Anniversary of the Journal of Negro History: Letters from Dr. Carter G. Woodson to Mrs. Mary Church Terrell," ed. by M. Sammy Miller. 61 (1976): 1-6.

An introduction to the letters stresses the importance of JNH as an achievement of Dr. Woodson's, identifies Mary Church Terrell, and pinpoints the purpose of the letters: to enlist her support for the JNH. The four letters (from the MS. division of the Library of Congress) follow.

BOOK REVIEWS BY WOODSON IN
THE JOURNAL OF NEGRO HISTORY

Woodson's book reviews express strong opinions of his contemporaries and the subjects and situations they deal with in their books. In them he sometimes writes a brief essay independent of his critique. To fully understand his thought on a variety of themes one must survey his book reviews.

46. Los Negros Esclavos. Estudios Sociologico y de Derecho Publico, by Fernando Ortiz. Havana, Cuba: Revista Bimestere Cubana, 1916. 3 (1918): 93-94.

   A contribution to scholarship in showing exactly how this institution affected the life and development of Cuba. Well illustrated with a valuable appendix of documents bearing on slavery in Cuba.

47. The Negro Migrant in Pittsburgh, a Study in Social Economics, by Abraham Epstein. Published under the supervision of the School of Economics, Univ. of Pittsburgh. Pittsburgh, Pa.: 1918. 3 (1918): 204-205.

   A scientific study of the transplanted southern Negroes, perhaps the first to appear in print. An interesting and valuable work.

48. The Negro in Literature and Art, by Benjamin Brawley. New York: Duffield and Company, 1918. 3 (1918): 329-30.

   The first work devoted to this aspect of Negro history; an interesting book which should attract all those who wish to understand the forces at work in the Negro mind and how they have found expression.

49. The Negro from Africa to America, by W.D. Weatherford, Ph.D., Pres. of the Southern College of YMCA. Introd. by James H. Dillard, Pres. of the Jeanes

Board and the John F. Slater Fund. New York: George H. Doran, 1924. 9 (1924): 574-77.

Woodson sees Dr. Weatherford as a man of good will making the effort to see the Negro as he is but says his book has many faults, undertaking too much and abounding in numerous long quotations followed by unwarranted conclusions. He calls the book a hodge-podge.

50. Brown America, by Edwin R. Embree. New York: Viking Press, 1931. 17 (1932): 114-15.

The author, a grandson of John G. Fee, a Kentucky abolitionist, treats of this crusader in the first part of the book which shows how brown Americans have developed in the United States and have achieved many things worthy of consideration.

51. White Spirituals in Southern Uplands, by George Pullen Jackson. Chapel Hill, N.C.: Univ. of North Carolina Press, 1933. 19 (1934): 93-96.

Woodson says that while science has been used to advance truth, it has also been used to advance untruth, as in the production of this book. The white man has not developed any such music as spirituals.

52. The Discovery and Re-discovery of America, by T.P. Christensen. Cedar Rapids, Ia.: Laurence Press Company, 1934. 20 (1935): 253-55.

This review is a characteristic example of Woodson's bitterness toward "Nordics" and authors whose books are written to supplant the achievements of Africans and Asians by those of "Nordics". Woodson claims that Chinese and Japanese had contacts with Africa thousands of years ago and that they touched America along the Pacific Coast.

53. Liberia in World Politics, by Nnamdi Azikiwe, Former Head of the Dept. of History and Political Science of Lincoln Univ., Pa. London: Arthur H. Stockwell, Ltd., 1925. 20 (1925): 351-53.

The author, a native African educated in the U.S., has treated Liberia sympathetically, saying that this last vestige of hope for African nationality should be safeguarded and revitalized.

54. The Education of the Negro in the American Social Order, by Horace Mann Bond. New York: Prentice-Hall, 1934. 20 (1935): 353-55.

Woodson condemns the book as unscientific, though he credits it as useful in a study of the history of education of the Negro. The book gives the impression that all that is needed is to remove the inequalities and everything will run along smoothly. Woodson says that educated blacks should be equal to demands for leadership.

55. <u>Negroes in the United States, 1920-1932</u>, comp. by Charles E. Hall, Specialist in Negro Statistics, asst. by Charles W. White of the U.S. Bureau of the Census in the Dept. of Commerce. Washington, D.C.: United States Government Printing Office, 1935. 20 (1935): 486-87.

Valuable facts brought together in a single volume in handy form.

56. <u>European Civilization, Its Origin and Development</u>, by various contributors, under the direction of Edward Eyre. Vols. I, II, and III. London: Oxford Univ. Press, 1934, 1935. 20 (1935): 487-88.

A monumental work under the direction of a distinguished man who sees history as it has been influenced by the Europeanization of the universe, produced with the cooperation of some of the greatest scholars of England. The work will consist of seven volumes. The Negro is mentioned casually among others in the treatment of world problems.

57. <u>Ethiopia, A Pawn in European Diplomacy</u>, by F. Ernest Work, published by the author and sold by the Associated Publishers. Washington, D.C., 1935. 20 (1935): 489-90.

The timely publication of this book fills a long-felt want especially in the United States where so little is known concerning ancient Ethiopia.

58. <u>Vers les Terres Hostiles de l'Éthiopie</u>, by Henry de Montfried. Paris: Editions Bernard Basset, 1933.
59. <u>Éthiopie, XXe Siecle</u>, by Henriette Celarié. Paris: Librarie Hachette, 1934.
60. <u>Les Flambeurs d'Hommes</u>, by Marcel Griaule. Introd. by S. Charléty. Paris: Calmann-Levy Éditeurs, 1935.
61. <u>L'Afrique Noire</u>, by Jacques Weulersse, Agrégé de l'Université. Paris: A. Fayard et Compagnie, 1934. 21 (1936): 78-83.

Woodson covers these four books in one review beginning with a survey of books on Ethiopia previously published. Henry de Montfried offers a book of travels which Woodson recommends for its vivid impressions of the author's observations. Celarié's work, also a travel book, takes up in detail the customs of the people and the relations of the tribes, especially the Somali and Danakils. Griaule's work is an account of a mission undertaken in 1928-29, a deeper and more scientific study than the previous two. The Weulersse volume is a broad geographical treatment.

62. Negro Musicians and their Music, by Maud Cuney-Hare. Washington, D.C.: Associated Publishers, 1936. 21 (1936): 220-21.

This is the first time a volume has been presented treating so thoroughly the music of the Negro, and presenting the philosophy underlying this contribution of the race. Though the author expresses more interest in art music than in folk music, she does not neglect the latter. The review gives some details of the author's life and of her research for the book.

63. Black and White in East Africa, The Fabric of a New Civilization, by Richard C. Thurnwald, with a chapter on "Women" by Hilde Thurnwald. London: George Routledge and Sons, 1935. 21 (1936): 221-23.

Though presented from the European view, the book contains valuable material and is more satisfactory than most books on Africa by European writers, though the European is still presented as a blessing coming to the "Dark Continent".

64. Something New Out of Africa, by H.W. New York: Pittman Publishing Corp., 1934. 21 (1936): 328-31.

The author traveled by plane over the continent and from these trips by air developed the book, which is merely another rehash of the imperialistic program. The theme of the book is advancing the defensive organization of the British Empire in Africa by air.

65. Consider Africa, by Basil Matthews. New York: Friendship Press, 1936. 21 (1936): 331-34.

The author assumes that the reader is familiar with the background of Africa which is undergoing changes from primitive conditions to industrialized life. From the tribal community system which has held the people together for a thousand years, workers have been drawn away into mines and factories. The European, interested only in increasing trade, has ignored the moral and material advancement of the natives.

66. Literature for the South African Bantu. A Comparative Study of Negro Achievement, by R.H.W. Shepherd, M.A. (Edinr.), Pretoria, S. Africa: The Carnegie Corporation Visitors' Grants Committee, 1936. 21 (1936): 334-36.

The author compares the achievements of the Bantu with those of the Negroes of the United States. He appraises the Negro in the United States much higher than most whites would do, and would encourage the Bantu to progress along the same lines. Bantu youth, he suggests, should be trained in research, the language should be standardized, and there should be more library service for the Bantu.

67. <u>Roger B. Taney</u>, by Carl Brent Swisher. New York: Macmillan Co., 1935.
68. <u>Roger B. Taney: Jacksonian Jurist</u>, by Charles W. Smith, Jr. Chapel Hill, N.C.: Univ. of North Carolina Press, 1936. 21 (1936): 438-43.

The review of these two books is an essay on Taney in which Woodson quotes from several other historians to defend his disagreements with the two authors. Swisher justifies Taney's course in the United States Bank question and in the Dred Scott decision as defensive in purpose and in keeping with his status as a member of the threatened landed aristocracy. Smith's book is worth reading, but some of his conclusions may seem self-contradictory. Rewriters of history must produce many more facts to give Taney a place among the great.

69. <u>A Brief Biography of Booker Washington</u>, by Anson Phelps Stokes. Hampton, Va.: Hampton Institute Press, 1936. 22 (1937): 108-109.

The brevity consists in selecting only a few aspects of Washington and omitting other significant ones. It throws some new light on his career because of the personal experiences of the author. The author overemphasizes the importance of Washington's dinner at the White House. While Roosevelt's importance is waning, Washington's increases as we review his achievement in education and world leadership.

70. <u>Horace Greeley and the Tribune in the Civil War</u>, by Ralph Ray Fahrney. Cedar Rapids, Ia.: Torch Press, 1936. 22 (1937): 109-12.

In this long review Woodson describes the book as a chapter in the history of the nation or the development of the press as a national force. The author reviews the work of newspapers which schooled Greeley in politics and ranks the <u>New York Tribune</u> above them all. Greeley's tendency was always to oppose Lincoln's policies. Though hostile to slavery he opposed employing military force to maintain the Union. Woodson finds much to praise in this book.

71. <u>A History of the South</u>, by William B. Hesseltine. New York: Prentice-Hall, 1936. 22 (1937): 240-46.

This book is a long step toward a well-balanced interpretation of the history of the South because it takes into account all the elements of the population rather than restricting the account only to whites. But Woodson takes exception to the author's reference to the Negro slave as under a patriarchial benevolence.

72. The Cape-to-Cairo Dream, by Lois A.C. Raphael. New York: Columbia Univ. Press, 1936. 22 (1937): 246-49.

This study of a further development of British Imperialism by the proposed railway to connect British possessions in South Africa with those in the Nile region is actually a tribute to Cecil Rhodes, not as a humanitarian but as an empire builder. The author takes no thought of the natives but brushes them aside as impediments encountered in the project. The book unconsciously presents the British Empire as doubtless the worst enemy in the world of the weaker races. The book is recommended to all those interested in the study of economic imperialism.

73. Negroes and the Law, by Fitzhugh Lee Styles. Boston: Christopher Publishing House, 1937.

74. Black Laws in Virginia, by June Purcell Guild. Richmond, Va.: Whittier and Shepperson, 1936. 22 (1937): 250-55.

The main purpose of Negroes and the Law is to present a summary of race distinctions in American law and to present to the public those Negroes who have battled against such barriers. Though the arrangement of materials is poor and there is no index the book renders a service in calling attention to Negro pioneers in the legal profession. Black Laws in Virginia shows that the present status of blacks may be explained by laws which have been enacted to deprive them of a chance to rise to the level of others. It excerpts from the laws of Virginia various measures enacted against slaves. Laws affecting free persons of color are in a separate section. Brought together are measures dealing with taxes, civil rights, criminal law, education, and military service, as they affected the Negro.

75. Life in a Haitian Valley, by Melville J. Herskovits. New York: Alfred A. Knopf, 1937. 22 (1937): 366-69.

The book helps to explain the composite culture in America. The author would not convey the impression that all transplanted blacks and their descendants are still Africans, but that this isolated community, because of being little influenced by European culture, offers an explanation of many other things where differences are less pronounced. Commenting on the final chapter, "Africa and Europe in Haiti," Woodson says that Dr. Herskovits departs from scientific standards, writing dogmatically his conclusions which may not be accepted as sound until further investigation.

76. Le Créole Haïtien, Morphologie et Syntaxe, by Suzanne Sylvain. (1936)

77. Les Créoles Haïtiens, Ire Partie. (1937)
78.   Les   Créoles   Haïtiens,   IIe Partie,   by   Suzanne
Comhaire-Sylvain.   Wetteren,   Belgium: Imprimerie   de
Meester, 1937.   22 (1937): 369-72.

The   language   of   the   Haitians   is   a   key to literary
treasures.   This   study   of   Haitian   folklore   was
presented   as   a   thesis   for   a   doctorate   at   the
Sorbonne.   After discussing the   structure   and   history
of   the   language,   the   author   concludes   that   the
languages of West Africa had a   prominent   influence   in
the   making   of   Haitian   Creole.   The   two   volumes   of
folklore have been gathered over many   years.   Vol.   II
centers   around   the   story   of the disguised animal and
the demon, presented   from   three   different   points   of
view.

79.   The   Civil   War   and   Reconstruction, by J.G. Randall.
New York: D.C. Heath and Co., 1937.   22 (1937): 372-77.

Since the author has used new sources   in   writing   this
book,   it   should   be   included,   in   spite   of   its
shortcomings, in the new historical   literature   of   the
United   States.   The   background   of   the   Civil War is
well portrayed, presenting   new   points   of   view   which
suggest   slightly   different   causes   of   the   conflict.
But   the   author   becomes   a   proslavery   defender.   The
long   book   contains   only   a   brief   treatment   of
Reconstruction.

80.   Judicial   Cases   Concerning   American   Slavery and the
Negro,   Volume   IV,   ed.   by   Helen   Tunnicliff   Catterall.
Washington,   D.C.:   Carnegie   Institution,   1936.   22 (1937):
377-79.

A valuable addition to   the   three   preceeding   volumes,
this   work   has   clarified the ante-bellum background in
American history by excerpting from printed   reports   of
cases   in   state   courts   and U.S. courts statements and
quotations illustrating slavery   and   the   life   of   the
Negro,   and   accompanying these by condensed versions of
applicable laws.   The   fourth   volume   deals   with   states
north   of   the   Potomac: Maryland,   the   District   of
Columbia, Delaware, the Middle States and New England.

81. Rhodes Goes North, by J.E.S.   Green.   London: G.   Bell
and Sons, 1936.   22 (1937): 379-82.

Under   Cecil   Rhodes   a   policy   of economic imperialism
developed   in   South   Africa   and   tactics   to   prevent
expansion   by   other   European   nations.   Green tells of
the   reaction   of   the   natives   to   the   explorers   and
missionaries, and   the   attitude   of   the   conquerer   to
those   already   occupying   the   land   as he attempted to
spread   transportation   facilities   and   to   exploit
resources.   Though   Rhodes   is   the outstanding figure in
the book, there is no hero worship of him.

82. Africans Learn to be French, by W. Bryant Mumford in consultation with Major G. St. J. Orde-Brown. London: Evans Brothers, 1937. 22 (1937): 494-96.

Almost half of the review is quoted from the book itself. The book is one of a series of surveys made by the Colonial Department of the University of London Institute of Education. The discussion of French educational organization is followed by a comparison of British and French methods, the author favoring British indirection over French direct rule.

83. Elizur Wright, The Father of Life Insurance, by Philip Green Wright and Elizabeth Q. Wright. Chicago: Univ. of Chicago Press, 1937. 22 (1937): 496-98.

The violent divisions of opinion relating to all abolitionists can be applied also to Elizur Wright. He combatted the idea of the exploiter and oppressor of every class. His range of interests was extremely wide and he had something to say on every one of them. A professor at Western Reserve College, Secretary of the American Anti-Slavery Society, and a writer of editorials in several newspapers, he achieved distinction as the Father of Life Insurance.

84. A Black Civilization, by W. Lloyd Warner. New York: Harper and Brothers, 1937. 22 (1937): 498-500.

The study of aborigines is a difficult task. They have few records. This book deals with a tropical Australian people, the Murngin tribe, and how they regulated their society and ritual. Anthropologists must decide upon the soundness of the conclusions Dr. Warner reaches from the analysis of the data he collected.

85. European Civilization; Its Origin and Development, by various contributors under the direction of Edward Eyre. London: Oxford Univ. Press, 1937. 22 (1937): 501-503.

These proposed seven volumes are a monumental work of history chiefly from a Catholic point of view. Volume V has more to say in respect to blacks than preceeding volumes. Woodson attributes the scanty references to blacks to the authors' being under the influence of the propaganda found in most of the recent histories bearing upon slavery and the Negro. References to racial history are chiefly in the article by Montague Fordham, "European Peasantry". Comparing the conditions of European peasants to those of the slaves from 1600 to 1914, the author considers the peasants in some cases freemen in name and slaves in fact.

86. A History of the State Teachers Association, by L.P. Jackson, Ph.D. Norfolk: The Guide Publishing Co., 1937. 23 (1938): 107-109.

Few Negro meetings have kept accurate records. Hence, this work which has drawn on the memories of still living members serves a great purpose. The names of outstanding educators appear, and problems which the Association had to meet, such as equal pay for equal work. Woodson mentions that the Virginia teachers have warmly supported the program of the Association for the Study of Negro Life and History.

87. The Negro and Crime in Virginia, by Bernard Peyton Chamberlain, of the Charlottesville and Albemarle County Bar. One of the Univ. of Virginia Phelps-Stokes Fellowship Papers. Charlottesville, Va.: Univ. of Va., 1937. 23 (1938): 109-11.

The author, writing with restraint and care but from incomplete data, has made some errors of judgment and fact while making an effort to be fair and to go to the root of the evil. He states that insurrections among slaves were few. He refers to Negro crime, though crime is not racial, and he suggests reforms.

88. Thomas Clarkson, The Friend of Slaves, by Earl Leslie Griggs. Ann Arbor: Univ. of Michigan Press, 1938. 23 (1938): 237-39.

Using valuable manuscripts in the possession of Clarkson's great-great-grand niece as well as MSS in English libraries, the author gives a clear picture of the crusader against slavery, and produces an informative work. The book is a tribute to the man who set up an organization which investigated the slave traffic and brought about the abolition of the trade by an act of Parliament in 1807.

89. The Cambridge History of the British Empire, Vol. VIII, South Africa, by J. Holland Rose, A.P. Newton, and E.A. Benians, gen. eds., and Eric A. Walker, Advisor in South Africa. Cambridge: at the Univ. Press, 1936. 23 (1938): 239-41.

This comprehensive study reviews the general history of Africa and then concentrates on the Cape and the gradual support given to Cecil Rhodes' Cape-to-Cairo program. Little is said about the natives' struggle to hold on to their land, but the book rather justifies questionable methods of exterminating the natives and becomes propaganda in favor of economic imperialism.

90. The Imperial Factor in South Africa, by C.W. De Kiewiet. Cambridge: at the Univ. Press, 1937. 23 (1938): 241-43.

Treats of the British Empire in South Africa in an analytical fashion, well-written and scholarly. The author has his own opinions on mooted questions much debated by authorities. He analyzes the blunders made by the British from the time they took over the Cape, their lack of understanding of the black man and their dependence upon black labor, raising problems far more pressing than republican independence or colonial self-determination.

91. <u>Renascent Africa</u>, by Nmamdi [sic] Azikiwe. Accra, Gold Coast, West Africa: Ziks Press, 1937. 23 (1938): 243-45.

The author, an African educated in the United States, established a newspaper in Accra to fight the battles of his people. In this book he goes far back in the early history of Africa and presents a whole picture of the natives in the grip of their conquerors. New Africa must win the contest through spiritual, social, and economic regeneration. The work invites attention to the present plight of the African natives and appeals to them for action in their own behalf.

92. <u>A History of Kentucky</u>, by Thomas D. Clark. New York: Prentice-Hall, 1937. 23 (1938): 245-46.

Woodson says there is no justification for writing histories of separate states, but that history should be approached by regions, and this author was not equal to his task. The conquest of the wilderness moved all pioneers beyond the mountains and what the author says of Kentucky is common to the larger region. The usual racial slant affected this author so that he refers to Negroes only in relation to slavery and labor.

93. <u>Southern Negroes, 1861-1865</u>, by Bell Irvin Wiley. New Haven, Conn.: Yale Univ. Press, 1938. 23 (1938): 370-71.

The author considers the Negroes' services to the ranking military on both sides in the Civil War, and also their conduct on plantations during the absence of their masters. The book has merit, though the author uses epithets, such as "darky", which are objectionable.

94. <u>Judicial Cases Concerning American Slavery and the Negro</u>, Vol. V, ed. by Helen Tunnicliff Catterall with additions by James J. Hayden. Carnegie Institution of Washington, D.C., 1937. 23 (1938): 371-72.

This is volume V of a work comprising a series of documents intending to show that the institution of slavery was actually like. Cases have been excerpted from state and from federal courts, accompanied by a statement of the respective law. This volume deals with Ohio, Indiana, Illinois, Michigan, Wisconsin,

Iowa, Missouri, Arkansas, Texas, Kansas, Nebraska, California, and also Canada and Jamaica, making available a wide body of source materials.

95. Lucretia Mott, by Lloyd C.M. Hare. New York: American Historical Society, 1937.   23 (1938): 372-74.

A Quaker who became a fearless reformer, Lucretia Mott was an agent in the Underground Railroad and a champion of woman suffrage.   The saintly woman who advocated abolition of slavery and braved persecution was loved and reverenced by the black people whose handicaps she labored to remove and to whom she devoted her life and energies.   Woodson calls the volume "gripping" and considers it valuable and scientifically written.

96. European Beginnings in West Africa, 1454-1578. Royal Empire Society Imperial Studies, No. 14, by J.W. Blake. London: Longmans, Green and Co., 1937.   23 (1938): 374-75.

European rivalry for control of African lands led to clashes between nations in trade and power.   The book serves as an introduction for wider study and provides a background, clarifying events which led up to the explorations undertaken by Christopher Columbus.   The natives are considered only as they stood in the way of European exploits.

97. Sojourner Truth, God's Faithful Pilgrim, by Arthur Huff Fauset. Chapel Hill, N.C.: The Univ. of North Carolina Press, 1938.   23 (1938): 375-76.

This book supplies a need for biographical material concerning prominent blacks, only a few of whom have had their careers recorded.   Fauset has written a readable story, which at times becomes gripping, about this strange figure so active in the anti-slavery struggle.   The book, though for the general reader not for the scholar, is yet timely and valuable.

98. The Negro College Graduate, by Charles S. Johnson. Chapel Hill, N.C. The Univ. of North Carolina Press, 1938.   23 (1938): 377-80.

Covers the time from the first black college graduate to the present, including careers and income, an impossible task even for a lifetime.   Thus the tables contain inaccuracies and the author makes mistakes in his historical background, classifying colleges incorrectly and misspelling names.   He attributes a college education to many who either did not attend college or who were there only a very brief time, and he considers as successful lawyers men who never practiced law.

99. <u>Thomas Paine: America's First Liberal</u>, by S.M. Berthold. Boston: Meador Publishing Co., 1938. 23 (1938): 487-89.

Woodson said he came slowly to an appreciation of Paine, without whom, someone said, we would not have had the American Revolution nor the Declaration of Independence. The review contains long quotations from famous men testifying to Paine's greatness, and quotations from Paine stating his ideals. His influence puts him in a class with George Washington and Thomas Jefferson. He exposed hypocrisy and worked untiringly for freedom and justice.

100. <u>The Negro in Economic Reconstruction</u>, by T. Arnold Hill.
101. <u>Negro Poetry and Drama</u>, by Sterling Brown.
102. <u>The Negro in American Fiction</u>, by Sterling Brown. Washington, D.C.: The Associates in Negro Folk Education, 1937. 23 (1938): 490-92.

Four of the series to which these three titles belong had already appeared and another was in preparation. They were designed for adult education. Before discussing the titles, Woodson comments unfavorably on the earlier ones, except for <u>World View of Race</u>, by Ralph Bunche. He praises Hill's pamphlet, though he says some of the language is difficult. The works by Sterling Brown are of interest to scholars and valuable contributions by a writer of depth and an able literary critic.

103. <u>William Alpaheus Hunton</u>, by Addie Waite Hunton. New York: Association Press, 1938. 23 (1938): 492-94.

Hunton was the pioneer who developed the Negro Department of the YMCA. He worked in Norfolk, Va., from 1888 until his death in 1916. His earlier life makes interesting reading. The book, however, fails to discuss the special problems of the Negro Department of the YMCA which Moorland and Hunton protested against.

104. <u>The Jew in the Medieval World, A Source Book, 315-1791</u>, by Jacob R. Marcus. Cincinnati, Oh.: The Sinai Press. 23 (1938): 494-95.

A selection of documents reflecting the history of the Jews, in three divisions: state, church, and home, as seen through the eyes of contemporaries, with little comment. In spite of disabilities and persecutions, the Jews survived. Woodson ends with a comparison between the oppressed Jew and oppressed blacks, very unfavorable to the black, to whom he attributes an inability to get rid of his inferiority complex.

105.   Africa's   God,   IX--South   Africa, by Joseph J.
Williams. Chestnut Hill, Mass.: Boston College Graduate
School, 1938.   23 (1938): 496-97.

Father Williams' series of monographs, except for the
earlier ones, are merely opinions which do not truly
present the mind of the African, and no better than
many other unsatisfactory works on the subject.
Woodson reproaches the author for referring to the
African's religion as superstition.

106. Dahomey, An Ancient West African Kingdom, by Melville
J. Herskovits. Two Volumes. New York: J.J. Augustin,
1938.   23 (1938): 497-99.

The introductory chapter of this work is a stimulating
discussion, especially Herskovits' evaluation of his
predecessors in the field. The work is, however, not
history, but cultural anthropology in which the author
is concerned with the economic and social life of
Dahomey as these relate to the internal structure and
organization of the kingdom. Though one who spends
only a short time in Africa can never know the African
mind, Herskovits has produced an interesting, though
incomplete, picture of Dahomey.

107. Le Trafic Negrier d'Après les Livres de Commerce du
Capitaine Gantois, Pierre-Ignace-Liévin Van Alstein, by
Père Dieudonné Rinchon, Capucin. Preface by M. Charles de
la Roncière, Conservateur à la Bibliothèque Nationale.
Brussels, Belgium: Editions Atlas and Paris: Librarie A.
Vanelsche 1938.   23 (1938): 499-500.

Dealing with the commercial organization of the slave
trade, which was considered an economic necessity,
this well-documented work, written from sources in
Nantes where the slave trade touched, excites horror
in the present day reader who has become more
sensitive than previous generations. Valuable
tabulations are included in the book, but the user
must remember that the work is restricted to the
participation of only certain Europeans.

108.   Juan Latino, Slave and Humanist, by V.B. Spratlin.
New York: Spinner Press, 1938.   24 (1939): 112-13.

Juan Latino and others were "taken from the wilds of
Africa" into the circles of the learned and proved by
their cultural achievements the mental capacity of the
Negro.   After summarizing Latino's career, especially
as a Latin scholar, Woodson praises Dr. Spratlin for
his scholarly work. The book contains in addition to
a biography of Juan Latino translations of some of his
work and critical comments.

109. Letters of James Gillespie Birney, 1831-1857, by Dwight L. Dumond. Two Volumes. New York: D. Appleton Co., 1938. 24 (1939): 113-14.

Birney, a slaveholder and legislator in Kentucky and a successful lawyer in Huntsville, Ala., changed his attitude in 1832, becoming first an agent for the American Colonization Society and later an abolitionist. In 1840 the Liberal Party he helped to form nominated him for president.

110. The American Race Problem. 2nd ed., rev. and reset, by Edward B. Reuter. New York: T.Y. Crowell Co., 1938. 24 (1939): 114-16.

Although Dr. Reuter discredits the idea of black inferiority as a theory never proved, his book is full of inconsistencies. He deplores the fact that black schools are passing into black hands. He assumes that the black has no history, and shows little knowledge of the African background.

111. Tell My Horse, by Zora Neale Hurston. Philadelphia: J.B. Lippincott Co., 1938. 24 (1939): 116-18.

Woodson praises Hurston for her work as an anthropologist and this book based upon her researches in Jamaica and Haiti. She participated in and learned firsthand of the primitive rites and customs she describes. The book is entertaining, but at the same time of value to scholars.

112. The Negro's God, by Benjamin E. Mays. Boston: Chapman and Grimes, 1938. 24 (1939): 118-19.

Mays, while reporting what Negroes themselves have said, speaks only for the literate. He divides his book into three epochs: slavery, reconstruction, and the period from then until World War I, showing the tendency toward change from one epoch to the next. The black's conception of God apparently reflects that of the white man.

113. The Negro in Brazil, by Arthur Ramos. Trans. from the Portuguese by Richard Pattee. Washington, D.C.: Associated Publishers, 1939. 24 (1939): 214-16.

The colonization program in Brazil was very different from that of the U.S., as the Latins, not planning permanent settlements, did not bring many women, and so produced mixed offspring who were accepted as citizens. This is a brief work which will prepare the way for fuller treatments.

114. Germans in the Cameroons, 1884-1914, A Case Study in Modern Imperialism, by Harry R. Rudin. New Haven, Conn.: Yale Univ. Press, 1938. 24 (1939): 217-19.

This book argues for the restoration of German imperialism in the Cameroons. The writer spent ten years in the country with access to German colonial records. He argues that if the Germans had not taken over the Cameroons, someone else less tolerent would have.

115. After Freedom, by Hortense Powdermaker. New York: Viking Press, 1939.   24 (1939): 219-20.

A sociological study of a backward Mississippi community which the author calls Cottonville. She refers to a process of acculturation in which the black learned behavioral patterns from the white man. Her sociological study uses history to illustrate certain points which have contributed to a new interpretation of southern history.

116. American Caste and the Negro College, by Buell G. Gallagher.   Foreward by William H. Kilpatrick. New York: Columbia Univ. Press, 1938.   24 (1939): 220-22.

The author sees caste as the key element through which the Negro college can function. The book is concerned with the application of known theories of social science to this idea as it presents the origin of caste and the dilemma of the system. The discussion is scholarly and sympathetic.

117. Two Quaker Sisters, Elizabeth Buffum Chase and Lucy Buffum Lovell, by Malcolm R. Lovell. Foreward by Rufus M. Jones. New York: Liveright Publishing Corp., 1937.   24 (1939): 222-23.

The author, a member of the family, has presented a family history which is also a contribution to Negro history because Quakers were strong and fearless champions of the cause of the Negro. These two sisters had the courage to fight publicly and to face the national government declaring the evils of slavery.

118. The Maroons of Jamaica, by Joseph J. Williams, S.J. Anthropological Series of the Boston College Graduate School. Boston: Boston College Press, 1938.   24 (1939): 224-25.

A documentary work consisting of quotations from other authors, government reports and laws, and the author's reports and comments on evidence of the transplanting of culture from the West Coast of Africa to America. A book of cultural anthropology, it supplements history and opens the way for historical treatment. The book should be widely circulated.

119. Thaddeus Stevens, by Alphonse B. Miller. New York: Harper and Brothers, 1939.   24 (1939): 351-53.

This biography, written in a scientific spirit and using an objective approach, is superior to previous biographies of Stevens. It may antagonize some historians by its advocating the cause of blacks. Sumner and Stevens promoted a plan which would have given true democracy to the South, but were refuted by the Reconstructionists.

120. To Make a Poet Black, by J. Saunders Redding. Chapel Hill, N.C.: The Univ. of North Carolina Press, 1939. 24 (1939): 356-57.

Redding has presented a brief history of black literature in which, he says, he does not apologize for the omissions, as they do not bear upon the trends and developments he wishes to demonstrate. While praising Redding's criticism of the authors he selected, Woodson faults him for presenting the mind only of the talented tenth.

121. Race, A History of Modern Ethnic Theories, by Louis L. Snyder. New York: Longmans, Green and Co., 1939. 24 (1939): 357-58.

This study of race is an historical survey which seeks to provide background for an understanding of Aryanism in the Third Reich and the adoption of a like policy in Italy. It describes race movements since the French Revolution and the ethnic theories which prompted them.

122. Crime and the Man, by Earnest Albert Hooton. Cambridge, Mass.: Harvard Univ. Press, 1939. 24 (1939): 359-60.

This primer of facts dealing with the anthropology of crime discusses the organic basis of crime and various classes of criminals. While the data show that blacks commit more robberies than whites, they also show that blacks commit fewer rapes than whites.

123. Bantu Heritage, by H.P. Junod. Johannesburg, S. Africa: Hortors, 1938. 24 (1939): 360-61.

Lectures given to acquaint members of the Transvaal Mine Medical Officers' Association with the culture and the mind of the Bantu as expressed in taboos, magic and religion. Not necessarily scientific, it aims to acquaint Europeans with these native Africans who must be understood if Africa is to be developed.

124. The Negro Immigrant, His Background, Characteristics and Social Adjustment, 1899-1937, by Ira De A. Reid. New York: Columbia Univ. Press, 1939. 24 (1939): 361-63.

This work is concerned with the 100,000 Negroes from

the West Indies, Canada and the Cape Verde islands who have immigrated to the United States, settling chiefly in New York and Florida. Statistics relate their place of origin, language, sex, marital status, etc. The immigrants' life story is written as a collective biography.

125. Black Folks Then and Now, by W.E.B. DuBois. New York: Henry Holt and Co., 1939. 24 (1939): 460-63.

Woodson complains that the treatment of Africa in this work is inadequate, failing to mention some important people and treating states of little importance as equal to greater. But he praises the section dealing with the New World after emancipation when capitalism continued the exploitation of blacks.

126. Black Workers and the New Unions, by Horace R. Cayton and George S. Mitchell. Chapel Hill,N.C.: The Univ. of North Carolina Press, 1939. 24 (1939): 463-64.

This last book of a series concerned with the New Deal program in relation to blacks shows how black industrial workers face problems in competition with whites organized by trade unions to prevent blacks from receiving equal pay and other benefits. Facts are presented from interviews with workers and officials throughout the country.

127. The Negro Family in the United States, by E. Franklin Frazier. Chicago: Univ. of Chicago Press, 1939. 24 (1939): 464-65.

In this comprehensive study almost every aspect of the Negro family is treated. Slavery and migratory movements are considered as they related to the stability of the black social organization; also urbanization, delinquency, and acculturation. Woodson disagrees with some of Frazier's conclusions in relation to the morals of the slaves.

128. The Growth of American Democracy, by Jeannette P. Nichols and Roy F. Nichols. New York: D. Appleton-Century Co., 1939. 24 (1939): 465-66.

The authors devote more than half the volume to the period since the Civil War, and devote little space to this conflict. Woodson faults their omission of blacks in their study except in relation to slavery, and their blaming blacks for the failure of Reconstruction.

129. Three Generations, by Charles W. Cansler. Knoxville, Tenn.: published privately by the author, 1939. 25 (1940): 108-109.

This autobiography is the history of a Negro family from the time of slavery to the twentieth century. Moving from North Carolina to Tennessee did not solve their problems and the Civil War added to them. References made to local and national events give the book value as history.

130. Gathered Fragments, by Bishop Randall Albert Carter. Nashville, Tenn.: The Parthenon Press, 1939. 25 (1940): 109-10.

This collection of thirty sermons and addresses by the Bishop of the Colored Methodist Episcopal Church is important and valuable for the light they will shed in future times on the period of history in which they were delivered, as well as because of the Bishop's standing as a national figure.

131. The Slavery Controversy, 1831-1860, by Arthur Young Lloyd. Chapel Hill, N.C.: Univ. of North Carolina Press, 1939. 25 (1940): 110-12.

A pro-slavery polemic almost totally ignoring the majority of anti-slavery workers whom the author brands as mar-plots and meddlers, communists and utopians. He questions the sincerity of the abolitionist who, he says, did nothing for the people. Woodson cites in refutation Prudence Crandall's school, Oberlin College, Oneida Institute and other benefactions.

132. Race Relations and the Race Problem. A Symposium on a Growing National and International Problem with Special Reference to the South, ed. by Edgar T.Thompson. Durham, N.C.: Duke Univ. Press. 25 (1940): 113-16.

Woodson briefly reports the thoughts of each member of the symposium and finds their theories contradictory in part. Among them Charles S. Johnson believes an increase in education will change the status of blacks; but, Woodson says, this will depend on the kind of education. Until these investigations are carried further they are not of much value.

133. The Course of the South to Secession, ed. by E. Merlton Coulter. New York: D. Appleton-Century Co., 1940. 25 (1940): 238-39.

A posthumous volume setting forth the last fully developed theory of the late U.B. Phillips. Although a defender of the South who considered slavery a beneficient institution, Phillips discovered new materials which can be used to present a less distorted picture than his. His latest theory was that the chief factors leading to secession were not economic and political, but psychological and racial.

134. Les Archives Privées et l'Histoire pour Connaître un
Type de Fortunes: Les Archives de Quelques Familles de
Planteurs Antillais, by G. Derbin. (A reprint from Annales
d'Histoire   Ecnomique   [sic] et Sociale.   Paris: Armand
Colin.)
135. Etude sur la Colonisation Française en Haïti, by
George-Ary Chevalier. Editions de la Societe d'Histoire et
de Geographie d'Haiti, 1938.   25 (1940): 240-41.

Though the first of these works is only six pages long
it is very informative regarding research materials to
be found in certain private archives.   The second is
an historical study of the French exploitation of the
West Indies, centered upon Haiti.   The author deals in
specifics not in generalizations.   Haiti, like the
other islands, had problems peculiar to itself rooted
in the early colonization period.

136. Haiti Singing, by Harold Courlander. Chapel Hill,
N.C.: Univ. of North Carolina Press, 1940.   25 (1940):
241-42.

This collection of Haitian folk songs is in their
original Creole and in English.   The appendix contains
the music of 126 of the 185 songs.   Covering a period
of four hundred years, from the beginnings of slavery
on the island, they show how certain blacks endeavored
to retain their African folkways.

137. Yearbook of Negro Churches, by Reverdy C. Ransom and
James H. Robinson. Philadelphia: A.M.E. Book Concern,
1939-40.   25 (1940): 378-79.

The foreward explains the dominance of the Church in
the life of the Negro, offering opportunities for
leadership and an outlet for expression in music and
art.   Though issued by the American Methodist
Episcopal Church, the volume includes data for the
YMCA, YWCA, National Association for the Advancement
of Colored People, and almost every other Negro
organization.   Woodson feels that the inclusion of
football stars and prize fighters is inappropriate.

138. Atticus Green Haygood, by Elam Franklin Dempsey.
Nashville, Tenn.: Parthenon Press, 1939.   25 (1940):
379-81.

Bishop Haygood of the Methodist Episcopal Church
South, because of his empathy with the Negroes in his
church, was selected to administer the Slater Fund
established to improve the condition of Negroes
through schools.   The book deals with his sermons,
letters, and the lives he influenced.   The loose
arrangement classifies it, not as a biography, but as
a source book.

139. <u>Haiti and the United States</u>, by Ludwell Lee Montague. Durham, N.C.: Duke Univ. Press, 1940. 25 (1940): 381-82.

Woodson summarizes the history of Haiti and its value to the United States for commercial reasons, and details the unsuccessful efforts of the Federal Government to obtain control of the island until the intervention of Wilson in 1915. Wilson sent in the Marines whose control encouraged cruelty and corruption. The author has used modern historiography in defense of a guilty Federal Administration.

140. <u>Old Sherry, Portrait of a Virginia Family</u>, by Frank J. Klingberg. Richmond, Va.: Garrett and Massie, 1938. 25 (1940): 382-83.

The history of the Wysor family through two generations reflects the history of the nation. The early members settled in a fertile valley in a slaveholding region and acquired the attitudes about them. Become stable members of society, they record their reactions to the crises of wars and the questions such crises raise.

141. <u>Joseph E. Brown and the Confederacy</u>, by Louise Biles Hill. Chapel Hill, N.C.: The Univ. of North Carolina Press, 1940. 25 (1940): 383-85.

The career of a governor of Georgia before and during the Confederacy; a biography rather than a political history. Brown considered states' rights more important than the demands of the Confederacy and refused to respect the quota of soldiers required by Jefferson Davis. Woodson says the struggle between Brown and Davis was "medieval" as were all slavocrats.

142. <u>The South to Posterity</u>, by Douglass Southall Freeman. New York: Charles Scribner's Sons, 1940. 25 (1940): 385-86.

While Freeman praises the inherent morale, military genius, and gallantry of the South and believes that the South leaves this tradition as an inheritance to all Americans, Woodson discredits his research, treatment and conclusions as propaganda written to support a certain point of view.

143. <u>The Negro in Congress</u>, by Samuel Denny Smith. Chapel Hill, N.C.: The Univ. of North Carolina Press, 1940. 25 (1940): 562-64.

The author, while presenting an extensive treatment of the subject, does not conceal his bias in several places, underrating the black statesman in regard to his understanding of national issues. He faults black legislators for harping on civil rights, the purpose for which they were in Congress.

144.   John   White   Geary,   by   Harry   Marlin   Tinkcom.
Philadelphia: Pennsylvania Univ. Press, 1940.   25 (1940):
564-65.

The book presents the career of a man who served in
the U.S. Army, took part in the California gold rush,
was Governor of the Territory of Kansas, and Governor
of the state of Pennsylvania. He was a strong
supporter of education for all children and of
compulsory school attendance.

145. The Economic Life of   Primitive Peoples, by Melville
J. Herskovits. New York: Alfred A. Knopf, 1940.   25
(1940): 566-67.

The author advances a new point of view and new
conclusions in anthropology in challenging some of the
former assertions of economics. Passing from the
purposes of tools discovered as evidence of the lives
of primitive people, he asks in regard to the potter
how his life was organized and what was the value or
gain from the finished product. The book challenges
economists and other anthropologists.

146. The Big Sea, An Autobiography, by Langston Hughes.
New York: Alfred A. Knopf, 1940. 25 (1940): 567-68.

Woodson highly praises this autobiography as well as
the work of Hughes as a poet as easily excelling most
of the contemporary poets of African blood. He never
drifted toward clownishness nor treated the black as
either totally a saint nor as a devil.

147.   Dusk   of   Dawn,   An Essay Toward an Autobiography of a
Race Concept, by W.E.B. DuBois. New   York: Harcourt,   Brace
and Co., 1940. 25 (1940): 568-69.

Though the biography spans three generations in the
life of a distinguished person, the work becomes
commentary and discussion of such subjects as race and
war, leaving the reader wondering about aspects of the
author's experiences never fully unfolded. He covers
ground he has been over before but broadens the
discussions from his contacts and experiences.

148. Gullah, Negro Life in the Carolina Sea Islands, by
Mason Crum of the Department of Religion, Duke Univ.
Durham, N.C.: Duke Univ. Press, 1940. 26 (1941): 117-18.

This valuable work although incomplete and not
strictly scientific, having been chiefly written from
secondary materials, nevertheless brings together
facts and materials previously available only in
scattered forms and contributes to an understanding of
the Negroes of the Carolina islands.

149.   A   Nickel   and   a   Prayer, by Jane Edna Hunter. Cleveland, Oh.: The Elli Kani Publishing Co., 1940.   26 (1941): 118-20.

Jane   Edna   Hunter   established   the   Phillis   Wheatley Association   in   Cleveland   to   provide   housing   and   a favorable   environment   for   the   poor   black   working girl.   Having   herself   experienced   the   difficulties these girls faced on coming into a new and strange city,   she   devoted   her   energies   to   combatting opposition,   and with "a nickel and a prayer" began the work.   This   book   is   her   autobiography   and   should inspire others to like achievements.

150.   Harlem: Negro Metropolis, by Claude McKay. New York: E.P. Dutton and Co., 1940.   26 (1941): 120-21.

This book   brings   fragmentary   materials   about   Harlem together   in   one   place.   Harlem   is no different from similar sections in any large city,   where   blacks   live by their wits.   Woodson would   like   a philosophical explanation for the existance   of   Harlem.   This   book, then,   though   interesting   reading,   serves   no   useful purpose.

151.   East   Africa   and its Invaders from the Earliest Times to the Death   of   Seyyid   Said   in   1856.   by   R.   Coupland. Oxford: The Clarendon Press, 1938.   26 (1941): 121-22.

After   the   collapse   of   the American colonies, Britain looked toward Africa for   expansion.   This   account   of her   exploitation   of East Africa gives only one side of the story, the British.   The African   and   Arab   stories are   left   untold   and the native African is disposed of in only a few pages.

152. The Exploitation   of   East   Africa,   1856-1890,   by   R. Coupland,   Beit   Professor   of Colonial History in the Univ. of Oxford.   London: Faber   and   Faber,   1939.   26   (1941): 122-23.

After   the   restriction   of   the   Arab   slave trade, the Europeans developed   a   new   system   of   exploiting   the natives   and   enriching   themselves   at   their   expense: economic   imperialism.   The   invasion   of Egypt and the scramble of European nations for parts   of   the   African land   led   to   plunder   and   a   different   kind   of enslavement.

153. Pushkin: A Collection of Articles   and   Essays   on   the Great   Russian   Poet.   Title   pages   and decorations by I.F. Rerberg.   Art ed.,   M.P.   Sokolnikov.   Moscow: The   U.S.S.R. Society   for   Cultural   Relations   with   Foreign   Countries, 1939.   26 (1941): 123-24.

A   collection   of   papers   in   honor   of   the   hundredth

anniversary of the death of Pushkin. An introduction
and a biographical essay are followed by discussions
of his contributions as the father of modern Russian
literature. The book justifies the claim that he
enriched Russian culture and presented to the world a
picture of Russian life.

154. A History of Freedom of Teaching in American Schools,
by Howard K. Beale. New York: Charles Scribner's Sons,
1941. 26 (1941): 265-66.

The evidence here shows little progress against
various forces operating against freedom of teaching.
A discussion of educational factors in historical
periods ends with industrialized America, 1917-1939.
The author discusses repression of ideas, pressure
upon teachers, and other such subjects. Education of
the Negro is given an important place.

155. The Story of the Negro, by Booker T. Washington. Two
volumes. New York: Peter Smith, 1940. 26 (1941): 266-67.

This is a reprint of a work published in 1909, and
constitutes economic and social history rather than
political history. Because of the prominance of
Booker T. Washington, there is demand for the work
which, Woodson says, supplements the larger work of
George Washington Williams.

156. Secret Societies: A Cultural Study of Fraternalism in
the United States, by Noel P. Gist. Columbia, Mo.: Univ.
of Missouri, 1899. 26 (1941): 267-68.

With an introduction by Melville J. Herskovits, the
volume deals with the culture which gave rise to
secret societies. Though Gist has not ignored the
influence of such organizations upon blacks and their
exclusion from most white societies, he has shown an
ignorance of the Negro's participation in the Masons
and the Odd Fellows.

157. Problems of Bantu Youth, by Ellen Hellman.
Johannesburg, S. Africa: South African Institute of Race
Relations, 1940. 26 (1941): 268-69.

Bantu youth leave school early for many reasons, among
them the instability of home life and a desire for
compensated employment. This is difficult to find
because of lack of schooling. The native is excluded
by law from the higher levels of employment and must
work long hours for little pay.

158. The Attitude of the Southern White Press Toward Negro
Suffrage, 1932-1940, ed. by Rayford W. Logan. Foreward by
Charles H. Wesley. Washington, D.C.: The Foundation
Publishers, 1940. 26 (1941): 269-70.

A small volume of excerpts from newspapers of twelve
southern states showing restrictions that prevent the
Negro from voting, which have included poll taxes,
literacy tests, property qualifications, registration
and residence restrictions and the White Primary. The
editor has included a resume of cases brought before
the Supreme Court to test the validity of the state
laws.

159. Education on an International Scale, by George W.
Gray. New York: Harcourt, Brace and Co., 1941. 26 (1941):
390-91.

The International Education Board funded by John D.
Rockefeller in 1923, during its fifteen years of
existance, promoted science and agriculture. The
Negro was sometimes the beneficiary as in African
colleges and Atlanta University. The need for such a
board is still very great.

160. Statistical Atlas of Southern Counties, ed. by
Charles S. Johnson. Chapel Hill, N.C.: The Univ. of North
Carolina Press, 1941. 26 (1941): 391-93.

The Council of Rural Education in 1934, financed by
the Rosenwald Fund, projected a survey of thirteen
southern states to determine conditions affecting
education. Included are thirty-six maps and tables
which cover every aspect of life in the counties where
Negroes live. Tabulations are given in
self-explanatory detail. A valuable volume.

161. The Economic History of Liberia, by George W. Brown.
Washington, D.C.: Associated Publishers, 1941. 26 (1941):
393-95.

A scientific study, without the sentimentality of many
previous books about Liberia, this work depicts early
Liberia as a dumping ground for emancipated Negroes
without experience or capital and describes the
European exploiters who took advantage of them. The
author exposes the mistakes the Liberians made.

162. Fearless Advocate of the Right, The Life of Francis
J. LeMoyne, M.D., 1798-1879, by Margaret C. McCulloch.
Boston: The Christopher Publishing House, 1941. 26
(1941): 395-97.

Dr. LeMoyne, a descendant of French emigres to Ohio, a
physician and frontiersman, kept alive the abolition
movement in western Pennsylvania where he established
himself after leaving Ohio. Active in the Underground
Railroad and working to secure national abolition, he
secured for Martin R. Delany admission to the Medical
College of Harvard.

163. The Negro in the Abolition Movement, by Herbert Aptheker. New York: International Publishers, 1941. 26 (1941): 401-403.

This short booklet shows what contribution Negroes themselves made to the abolition movement. Blacks are not given much credit for aiding in securing their rights and freedom, but Aptheker produces facts to show that blacks were the first abolitionists and were actively struggling for the destruction of slavery in the ante-bellum period.

164. Anglican Humanitarianism in Colonial New York, by Frank J. Klingberg. Philadelphia: The Church Historical Society. 26 (1941): 529-30.

Dr. Klingberg used the records of the Society for the Propagation of the Gospel in Foreign Parts to show humanitarian achievement in the eighteenth century in Great Britain and colonial New York. Because of the tradition that Christians could not be held slaves, colonists were adverse to the idea of converting blacks.

165. The Northern Teacher in the South, 1862-1870, by Henry Lee Swint. Nashville, Tenn.: Vanderbilt Univ. Press, 1941. 26 (1941): 531-33.

Since the author has a southern bias, this book is without the detachment necessary for a fair picture. His point of view is that the teachers had political and self-serving motives for coming. Southerners rejected and insulted them. The South, he says, did not object to the education of Negroes, but only to their being taught by Yankees.

166. The Present State of Virginia, and the College, by Hartwell, Blair and Chilton. Williamsburg, Va.,: Colonial Williamsburg, Inc., 1940. 26 (1941): 534-36.

This book, a reprint of a history of Virginia written in 1692, showing what the colony had become ninety years after its founding, is a report to the Board of Trade in London. The historical background mentions tobacco growing with slave labor and endeavors to explain the economic forces in America.

167. The Colour Bar in East Africa, by Norman Leys. London: The Hogarth Press, 1941. 26 (1941): 538-39.

Norman Leys, who in other works has shown the injustices of the British toward natives, shows that the color bar in East Africa is as bad as in South Africa where it borders on medieval cruelty. He discusses how the color bar developed gradually without the sanction of Parliament and without British statesmen knowing about it.

168. Native African Medicine, With Special Reference to its Practice in the Mano Tribe of Liberia, by George Way Harley, M.D. Cambridge, Mass.: Harvard Univ. Press, 1941. 26 (1941): 539-40.

Dr. Harley shows that medicine in the Mano tribe is distinguished from religion. Though disease is considered the work of evil forces, the Mano use rational remedies as distinct from magical ones. At times they may use both. Evidence shows valuable remedies in African medical practice.

169. Boston's Immigrants, 1790-1865, A Study in Acculturation, by Oscar Handlin. Cambridge, Mass.: Harvard Univ. Press, 1941. 27 (1942): 109-11.

This study traces the population of Boston from 1790 to the end of the Civil War when it took on its present aspect. The largest contingent of foreign population was Irish which clashed with Negro workers in competition for jobs. Bostonians were more concerned about the Irish against whose Catholicism they had strong religious prejudices than about blacks.

170. Lincoln and the Radicals, by T. Harry Williams. Madison, Wisc.: Univ. of Wisconsin Press, 1941. 27 (1942): 111-14.

An interesting and stimulating book which portrays the dissentions with which Lincoln had to contend in wartime administration. Most of the generals of the Army were Northern Democrats trained at West Point, who were not interested in the immediate destruction of slavery, but only wished to preserve the Union. The "radicals" worked to displace them.

171. Shop and Classes at Tuskegee, by J. L. Whiting. Boston: Chapman and Grimes, 1941. 27 (1942): 114-15.

This book describes the work and courses at Tuskegee from 1919-1930, and gives the author's views on vocational education. He relates some of Booker T. Washington's and his experiences. Though the book contains valuable information for those interested in this type of instruction, it is badly organized.

172. The Myth of the Negro Past, by Melville J. Herskovits. New York: Harper and Brothers, 1941. 27 (1942): 115-18.

Some writers have supported the erroneous theory that blacks brought nothing from Africa but their temperament. These, however, are neither historians nor anthropologists. Dr. Herskovits shows that black Americans differ from other Americans due to early African influences. He has uncovered facts to show that African survivals are present.

173. <u>The Republic of the United States, A History</u>. Volume I, by Jeanette P. Nichols and Roy F. Nichols. New York: D. Appleton and Co., 1942. 27 (1942): 231-32.

The aspect of Republic in this volume relates to the way in which Americans have learned to govern themselves. While the authors deal with some events which other histories ignore, they do not sufficiently consider the slavery question and the situation of blacks, though they do show some relation between these questions and contemporary problems.

174. <u>Northern Editorials on Secession</u>, comp. by Howard Cecil Perkins. Two volumes. New York: D. Appleton-Century Co., 1942. 27 (1942): 232-33.

The book contains 495 of the most representative editorials appearing from September 1860 to 1861, from all the free states and all political parties. The compiler considers that secession had been under discussion from the beginning of the country until the crisis. The volume shows what people were saying--often without thinking--during that time.

175. <u>Guinea's Captive Kings</u>, by Wylie Sypher. Chapel Hill, N.C.: The Univ. of North Carolina Press, 1942. 27 (1942): 234-35.

As further research was prevented by the war, the author decided to give to the public his unfinished study. He presents the development of British anti-slavery thought in the literature of the empire, making detailed examination of literary expression in legend, verse, drama, and fiction.

176. <u>Howard University, The Capstone of Negro Education</u>, by Walter Dyson. Washington, D.C.: The Graduate School, Howard Univ., 1941. 27 (1942): 235-36.

The author of this volume, an instructor in history at Howard University, presents its story from its beginnings under its founder General Oliver Otis Howard to its expansion which included the professional schools of religion, law, and medicine. Woodson considers Howard's real contribution to be the large number of useful doctors and lawyers the university has supplied.

177. <u>Shakespeare in Harlem</u>, by Langston Hughes. New York: Alfred A. Knopf, 1942. 27 (1942): 236-37.

A distinguished poet's first book of poems in ten years reveals the same theme as before but in more mature verse. Woodson considers the Harlem tradition overemphasized but sees these poems as the black man's appeal for justice. He characterizes Langston Hughes as a good poet and a soldier for human rights.

178. The Biology of the Negro, by Julian Herman Lewis, Ph.D., M.D. Chicago: The Univ. of Chicago Press, 1942. 27 (1942): 359-61.

A welcome volume by an authority in pathology, both scientific and historical. It discusses theories advanced from time to time which have affected attitudes and policies toward blacks. Before taking up specific diseases the author dissects the black man anatomically. That reaction to disease is a racial characteristic is sustained by investigation.

179. Louisiana in the Confederacy, by Jefferson Davis Bragg. Baton Rouge, La.: Louisiana State Univ. Press, 1942. 27 (1942): 361-63.

The history of the Confederacy can be known through the history of any one state, but the author feels that Louisiana is different because it was early under Federal control. There is some new light on social and economic conditions, and the book is written with some restraint, though influenced by Claude Bowers, the master propagandist.

180. Forward the Nation, by Donald Culross Peattie. New York: G.P. Putnam's Sons, 1942. 27 (1942): 363-64.

Peattie's treatment of the westward expansion and the Lewis and Clark Expedition is disappointing but his delineation of the romantic figures is dramatic and he gives the Indians important treatment. The blacks who participated in the venture, however, are treated only as equipment, even though Pompey, who died on the way, gave his name to Pompey's Pillar, a post office in Montana.

181. Slave Songs of the Georgia Islands, by Lydia Parrish. Intro. by Olin Downes. New York: Creative Age Press, 1942. 27 (1942): 465-67.

The author lived among the black people of the Georgia Islands for twenty-five years recording their songs and folkways. She interprets their philosophy of life, showing through their music how and why they differ from other American blacks. Her methods meet scientific standards, though scientists will hardly agree with all her conclusions.

182. American Negroes, A Handbook, by Edwin R. Embree. New York: The John Day Co., 1942. 27 (1942): 467-68.

The author does not present anything new in this short work but gives the public in succinct form the facts from his Brown America, in the hope that the shorter work will find readers which the longer might intimidate. He believes that democracy in this

country is progressing and that blacks will eventually
be respected as citizens.

183. Welcum Hinges, by Bernard Robb. Illus. by Woodi
Ishmael. New York: E.P. Dutton and Co., 1942. 27 (1942):
470-72.

This book, idealizing slavery and lamenting the Lost
Cause, makes inconsistent statements as when Robb
characterizes the slave as lazy, then tells how the
sick slave refused to stay in bed and be nursed, but
insisted on getting up to attend to his work. The
book is intended to glorify the slaveholder and to
make heroes of those who attempted to destroy the
Union.

184. Negroes in Brazil, by Donald Pierson. Chicago: The
Univ. of Chicago Press, 1942. 27 (1942): 474.

This work is somewhat misnamed, treating only of
Bahia, but it supplements the work of Arthur Ramos,
The Negro in Brazil. It covers the slave trade, its
operation and destruction, as well as religious
practices. The author finds African survivals fast
disappearing. He is concerned with ethnic composition
of classes and racial attitudes. A valuable volume.

185. Storm over the Land, A Profile of the Civil War, by
Carl Sandburg. New York: Harcourt, Brace and Co., 1942.
28 (1943): 88-90.

An abridgement of the author's Abraham Lincoln: The
War Years, which should add much to his popularity.
Though the author does not discuss politics there is
no doubt of the stand of statesmen on both sides. He
tells his story around significant encounters and
events. Blacks figure as persons and participants in
the drama.

186. Sex and Race, Volume I, by J.A. Rogers. New York:
J.A. Rogers Historical Researches, 1942. 28 (1943): 91-92.

This volume treats of race admixture in the Western
Hemisphere. The first part deals with the fusion of
Negro, Indian and Caucasian in Latin America; the
second with the United States. The author discusses
the breakdown of preventive legislation, concubinage
and intermarriage, noting famous white Americans of
black ancestry.

187. Fair Play, by Henry Noble MacCracken and Charles
Gordon Post. Poughkeepsie, N.Y.: Vassar College, 1942.
    Race and Cultural Relations, by Ruth Benedict and
Mildred Ellis. Washington, D.C.: National Education
Association, 1942. 28 (1943): 93-94.

Both pamphlets are significant. Fair Play comes from Vassar College which until recently refused admittance to blacks. Excuses are offered for past inhumanity. The work has historical value as a review of unfair practices and discrimination. Race and Cultural Relations offers a method of undoing the evil of centuries, but displays an ignorance of black history and the past achievements of blacks.

188. Une Plantation de Saint-Dominique, La Sucrerie Galbaud du Fort, 1690-1802, by G. Debien. Cairo, Egypt: L'Institut Français d'Archéologie Orientale du Caire, 1942. 28 (1943): 94-96.

The data for this scholarly monograph were collected from official papers and plantation records. The vicissitudes of establishing the plantation, the development of slave labor and the international competition for sugar all played a part in creating a rich French colony. The records expose the inhumanity of slavery even more than the revelations of reformers.

189. The Union's Burden of Poverty, by J.D. Rheinalt Jones and R.F. Alfred Hoernelé. Johannesburg, S. Africa: South African Institute of Race Relations, 1942.
190. The Basis of Trusteeship, by J.C. Smuts. Johannesburg, S. Africa: South African Institute of Race Relations, 1942.
191. Labour and the New Economic Policy, by Eleanor Hawarden. Johannesburg, S. Africa: South African Institute of Race Relations, 1942.
192. Cape Coloured People To-day, Vol. IX, No. 1 of Race Relations, by various contributors. Johannesburg, S. Africa: South African Institute of Race Relations, 1942.
193. Political Representation of Africans, by various contributors. Johannesburg, S. Africa: South African Institute of Race Relations, 1942. 28 (1943): 96-100.

These pamphlets in a series are concerned with questions which the war has forced South Africa to examine. The whites force into the submission of serfs the native four-fifths of the population, who for the most part live in poverty. The writers neither defend the natives nor plead their cause but propose programs to follow which may benefit all the population, and present recommendations from various aspects.

194. Jefferson Himself, by Bernard Mayo. Boston: Houghton Mifflin Co., 1942. 28 (1943): 240-42.

Mayo compiled an "autobiography" of Thomas Jefferson from letters, papers and documents to give a complete picture of the man. Woodson objects that such a portrait cannot be true, as a person's attitudes change with circumstances. In discussing this book's shortcomings, Woodson presents an admiring essay on Thomas Jefferson.

195. <u>Old Thad Stevens</u>, by Richard Nelson Current. Madison, Wisc.: The Univ. of Wisconsin Press, 1942. 28 (1943): 243-46.

The author had the advantage of documents previously unused. His data are used only to discredit Stevens as a statesman and present him as an ambitious politician. Woodson refutes the unflattering assertions of the author, saying Current looked for two things only: politics and filth, and he accuses him of suppressing material which did not fit the picture he wished to present.

196. <u>Lincoln and his Party in the Secession Crisis</u>, by David M. Potter. New Haven, Conn.: Yale Univ. Press, 1942. 28 (1943): 246-48.

This book sets out to prove that the Civil War need not have happened, and to show that the problems involved could have been settled in conference. Woodson says that the conflict that had been brewing for forty years was inevitable and would have occurred even if Lincoln had never lived, but the nation was fortunate to have his wisdom when it finally came.

197. <u>The Hidden Civil War</u>, by Wood Gray. New York: Viking Press, 1942. 28 (1943): 249-51.

In this valuable book the author shows the crises through which Lincoln had to go under the stress of the Civil War: secret opposition to the war and attempts to prevent enlistments, the activities of the Copperheads and the lack of united strategy of the Union Generals, who resented that a man who was not a seasoned soldier should interfere in military matters.

198. <u>The Disarmament Illusion</u>, by Merze Tate. New York: The Macmillan Co., under the auspices of the Bureau of International Research of Harvard Univ. and Radcliffe College, 1942. 28 (1943): 251-53.

Dr. Tate's book is evaluated as a gripping yet scientific treatment of what nations did for and against disarmament during the period 1870-1907. While statesmen conferred over the subject and appeared as humanitarians their objectives were really the balance of power or maintaining the status quo.

199. <u>Joseph Charles Price</u>, by William Jacob Walls, Bishop of the African Methodist Episcopal Zion Church. Boston: Christopher Publishing House, 1943. 28 (1943): 355-56.

Thinker, orator, founder of Livingstone College, Price

was a leader in education and race relations. The author does not do him justice, touching on and developing so many other things that Price is lost in the myriad of facts. Yet Bishop Walls has assembled materials throwing light on the past of blacks, especially in North Carolina.

200. <u>George Washington Carver</u>, by Rackham Holt. New York: Doubleday, Doran Co., 1943. 28 (1943): 358-60.

Mrs. Holt's dramatic biography tells of Carver's heroic efforts to obtain an education, while it also shows his interests in other things such as knitting, cooking, baseball and painting. The author treats more deeply of Carver as a scientist. He early understood that there is nothing ugly and useless in nature if one would appeal to it for what it has in store.

201. <u>A History of Oberlin College from its Foundation through the Civil War</u>, by Robert S. Fletcher. Two Volumes. Oberlin, Oh.: Oberlin College, 1943. 28 (1943): 360-362.

Written by a Professor of Oberlin, these two volumes will give the noted college its place in history. The work is divided into five books, relating the opening of the institute and its attitude of emancipation and women's equality. Its liberalism accepted not only women along with men, but also blacks. It was one of the important stations on the Underground Railroad. Through hard times and tribulations religious reformers advocated labor and learning as students worked their way from elementary subjects to the college and theology. Oberlin can claim priority in many spheres, among them its conservatory of music and the first black woman college graduate (1862) in America.

202. <u>Records of the Moravians in North Carolina</u>, Volume VI, <u>1793-1808</u>, by Adelaide L. Fries, Archivist of the Moravian Church in America, Southern Province. Raleigh, N.C.: The North Carolina Historical Commission, 1943. 28 (1943): 360-362.

While the records of a minority group like the Moravians will seem boring to a lay person, historians find valuable and gripping material in such narratives. The Moravians are especially interesting, having conquered the wilderness of North Carolina and set up a religious settlement. They sheltered run-away slaves and received twenty-eight into the community. Woodson says these records show how difficult has been the effort to make Christianity conform to the principle of the brotherhood of man and the fatherhood of God.

203. <u>Horse and Buggy Days with Uncle Sam</u>, by John H. Paynter. New York: The Margent Press, 1943.   28 (1943): 362-63.

> John H. Paynter, a descendant of one of the old families of Washington, after serving in the U.S. Navy, became a clerk in the U.S. Department of Internal Revenue. The author of other works, including the <u>Fugitives of the Pearl</u>, he adds to his renown with this volume. It contains an account of the relations of the races before segregation tendencies developed under Taft and were systemized under Wilson. He saw the change from "equality to toleration and next from toleration to hostility" when blacks were appointed only to drudgery, and only whites to clerical positions.

204. <u>Forced Labour</u>, by C.W.W. Greenidge. London: The Aborigines Protection Society, Denison House, 1943.   28 (1943): 363-65.

> Though but a pamphlet this significant work points out that the British Empire resorts to forced labor in Kenya and in Nigeria, although measures have been placed on the International Statute Book of the International Conventions of Labour (1930-1939). The steps taken by these conventions to outlaw forced labor are reviewed. Laborers between the ages of 18 and 55 are conscripted to the tin mines of Nigeria, all native Africans. Woodson compares this situation with labor in the Cotton Belt of the United States, "secured mainly by peonage and sharecropping."

205. <u>The Negro in Colonial New England, 1620-1776</u>, by Lorenzo Johnston Greene. New York: Columbia Univ. Press, 1942.   28 (1943): 478-81.

> Dr. Greene's serious treatment of colonial Rhode Island and Massachusetts follows a scientific method to expose the other side of the question which pro-slavery historians have been playing up for decades. Slavery was legally established in Massachusetts in 1641 and, though New England never had many blacks, the colonies grew rich on the slave trade. Slave traders were heads of the best families who made their fortunes in "Black Merchandise." On the eve of the American Revolution slave trade was the basis of economic prosperity of New England, especially Rhode Island and Massachusetts. The book touches on the social life, labor, punishments of slaves and legal proscriptions for both slaves and free blacks. Woodson's review is an extensive essay.

206. <u>The Free Negro in North Carolina, 1790-1860</u>, by John Hope Franklin. Chapel Hill, N.C.: The Univ. of North Carolina Press, 1943.   28 (1943): 482-85.

Woodson has great praise for Dr. Franklin's work as a scientific study containing many surprises; among them that in early North Carolina intermarriage and voting were practiced by blacks and that the outstanding teacher of the time was black John Chavis, whose school was attended by both black and white children. As prejudice increased liberalism was crushed. People felt threatened by Nat Turner's insurrection in nearby Virginia. Woodson regrets that Franklin did not treat further of the Indians nor of the effect of the anti-slavery movement on the free blacks. He asks if the Northwest migration (1815-1840) aided by liberal-minded Quakers affected the conditions of the free blacks.

207. The South in American History, by William B. Hesseltine. New York: Prentice-Hall, 1943. 28 (1943): 485-88.

In this new edition of The History of the South (1936) the author, though born in the South, is not a partisan nor a progagandist. For his new edition he consulted professors of history in several southern universities. Disagreements always arise as to what should be included in a one-volume history where nothing can be treated in detail. The author in general has been unbiased in his treatment of blacks, going beyond what most previously published histories have contained to show the presence of this part of the population. Some of the faults and errors of the earlier edition still remain, especially regarding blacks during reconstruction but this is a search for truth, not "history made to order."

208. Jim Crow's Last Stand, by Langston Hughes. New York: Negro Publication Society of America, 1943. 28 (1943): 492-94.

A slender volume of 29 poems, No. 2 of the "Race Culture Series" deals with democracy and freedom, and conditions which thwart the efforts of blacks for better living, ending in an optimistic vein with "Jim Crow's Last Stand." Woodson, looking back over seventy years traces the progress of blacks toward true independence: nominal freedom after emancipation, re-enslavement by the black codes, federal reconstruction to protect blacks followed by withdrawal of troops and the status of chattel slavery once again, the awakening after World War I, and today a more aggressive step toward world brotherhood as blacks present their "case before a new tribunal."

209. Five French Negro Authors, by Mercer Cook. Washington, D.C.: Associated Publishers, 1943. 28 (1943): 494-97.

Dr. Cook has rendered the serious-minded students of our present world problems a service by presenting five men from the West Indies who have achieved distinction by their writings: the well-known Alexandre Dumas, Rene Maran who won the Goncourt prize for his Batoula, Julien Raimond, Cyrille-Charles-Auguste Bisette, and Auguste Lacaussade. They did not all think alike, but each reflects the aspirations and feelings of his time. These accounts reveal the policies of the mother country toward Haiti, Guadeloupe, and Martinique and the fundamentals of French colonial history.

210. Race and Rumors of Race, by Howard W. Odum. Chapel Hill, N.C.: The Univ. of North Carolina Press, 1943. 29 (1944): 92-94.

Dr. Odum sees a crisis in the upset of jimcrow which has disturbed the southern calm. The dangerous situation is made worse by rumors which show the country standing over a volcanic explosion threatened by aggressive Negroes who will not be "Uncle Toms." Woodson calls Odum's "affectionate appeal" for a new covenant through scientific and cooperative endeavor beautiful words. He refers sarcastically to the social scientist who by a simple formula will settle a brawl so long brewing. Woodson says only by the shedding of blood will the southern white be dislodged from his position of supremacy and he quotes Thomas Jefferson in his support.

211. A Handbook of the Detroit Negro, by Ulysses W. Boykin. Detroit, Mich.: The Minority Study Associates, 1943. 29 (1944): 94-96.

While Mr. Boykin has not shown the ability to treat his facts in a scientific fashion, he is the forerunner who deserves credit for telling the story of the Negro in Detroit. He has brought out some new facts, particularly by rescuing from oblivion some black leaders of Detroit. This modest production is very welcome.

212. Main Currents in English History, by Frank J. Klingberg. New York: D. Appleton-Century Co., 1943. 29 (1944): 96-98.

A handy and timely volume to have in the midst of a war in which English civilization is at stake, the author deals not only with origins but also treats in some respects with the subordinated peoples of the British Empire. The book presents the strong and weak elements of British government. Woodson asks: Can the English nation learn to place human rights above property? This, he says, is the unsolved problem of the English system of government.

213. <u>George Fitzhugh, Propagandist of the Old South</u>, by Harvey Wish. Baton Rouge, La.: Louisiana State Univ. Press, 1943. 29 (1944): 98-101.

A narrow-minded man, knowing or understanding little about history, Fitzhugh offered a program to the South in imitation of Greek democracy based upon perpetual Negro slavery. Dr. Wish points out Fitzhugh's fallacies which aligned him with contemporary Fascism. One learns from the book how southern writers defending slavery influenced and supported one another. Though Fitzhugh changed his point of view somewhat after Emancipation he never departed from his plantation philosophy.

214. <u>Negro Musicians and their Music</u>, by Maud Cuney-Hare. Washington, D.C.: Associated Publishers, 1943. 29 (1944): 101-103.

The author, a widely-traveled trained musician "conducted" this work "on the scientific order." Besides recording the achievements of black musicians she points out the fallacy of the claim that the spirituals, the jubilees and jazz originated with whites, and leaves these "traducers exposed to serious charges." At the time Woodson wrote this review the book had already been through three printings and was in its second edition. The book, he says, is a fine tribute to the author who gave "so much for the country ... when it gave her so little."

215. <u>Modern Negro Art</u>, by James A. Porter. New York: The Dryden Press, 1943. 29 (1944): 231-33.

Though recent discoveries of high artistic merit have been made in Africa, the author has not dwelt on those but has indicated achievements of craftsmen and artists of pre-Civil War days and later in America. After Emancipation, with the beginning of the century, painters and sculptors developed whose works ranked with the best. African art has been exerting increased influence on Afro-American artists.

216. <u>Characteristics of the American Negro</u>, by Otto Klineberg. New York: Harper and Brothers, 1944. 29 (1944): 233-36.

Klineberg, in this last volume of <u>The Negro in American Life</u> series from a grant made to Gunner Myrdal, takes up where Howard W. Odum left off, and does better than his predecessor in not labeling environmental habits and customs in blacks as racial characteristics. Being white he cannot study black characteristics from within, but he has done as well "as the Negro scholar who has been misled ... in some of our graduate schools." Myrdal, a foreigner of limited contact with blacks, has produced an incomplete picture, and Woodson further says, a large mass of data he has collected has not been used in the survey. This long review continues with evaluations of other books in the survey, for the most part uncomplimentary.

217. Las Culturas Negras en el Nueva Mundo, by Arthur Ramos. Mexico City, Mexico: Fondo de Cultura Economica, 1943. 29 (1944): 236-38.

The author's interest in anthropology has led him to explore the observations and theories of anthropologists who have worked in various areas of the Americas. His limited knowledge of North America makes this his weakest section. He quotes excellent authorities for Cuba, Haiti, the Bahamas, and the Guianas. The rest of South America is sketchy except for Brazil which, as a native, he knows well and has written about in The Negro in Brazil. The present volume is evidence that little is known about blacks in most parts of South America. Dr. Ramos has rendered a great service.

218. Freedom's Ferment, by Alice Felt Tyler. Minneapolis, Minn.: The Univ. of Minnesota Press, 1944. 29 (1944): 383-85.

The book serves well the cause of historical interpretation in a readable volume. It points out the unifying influence of reform movements, one movement (temperence) encouraging another (women's rights). Many of these efforts were inconsistent or illogical, but they forced upon the public the need for change. The initiators often did not live to see the effects of their efforts, but their successors brought about social and political reforms. Woodson praises the work, though the author did not give enough credit to blacks for their part in the abolition movement. He ends his review by summarizing the initiative of blacks in abolition and the Civil War.

219. Middle America, by Charles Morrow Wilson. New York: W.W. Norton and Co. 29 (1944): 385-87.

Woodson disagrees with the author's premises that the introduction of scientific agriculture and education into Central America, Cuba, Haiti, and the Dominican Republic by the United States would be welcomed by those living there. The author wishes to encourage such activity for commercial competition and international relations. Woodson points out that our efforts (at the point of a bayonet) have been tried and failed in Haiti. He feels that the author needs more knowledge of the social and political handicaps to be removed.

220. Libro de la Primera Reunion de Professores Universitarios Espanoles Emigrados. Talleres Tipograficos "Le Mercantil," Palacio y Compania, Brasil, nos. 54-56. Havana, Cuba, 1944. 29 (1944): 387-89.

Present at the conference for exiled Spanish scholars in Havana were professors and others from various countries. It is not known, Woodson says, whether representatives from black universities in the United States were invited; they could have impressed the foreign scholars with their "real worth." Radical changes are being advocated by thinkers who realize we shall never enjoy peace until there is a break with the past. Probably they said little about the rights of races because they recognize people for their worth. They have no such tribalism as that so dear to the people of the United States.

221. Know Your Enemy, by T.H. Tetens. Intro. by Emil Ludwig. New York: The Society for the Prevention of World War III, 1944. 29 (1944): 389-91.

These documents from German writings which have shaped the thought of that country contain what may be considered by many as propaganda. The compiler hopes they may influence leaders sufficiently to prevent another world war. The interpretation given these documents may increase bitterness against Germany and cause a demand for greater reparations, impossible for the nation to discharge. Woodson says instead of worrying about Germany we should be thinking about how to curb the victorious British from getting a stranglehold of the entire modern world.

222. A Faith to Free the People, by Cedric Belfrage. New York: The Dryden Press, 1944. 29 (1944): 484-85.

This biography of Claude Williams portrays a man of courage and conviction who, in spite of trials and persecutions, endeavors to restore the common people's faith in the principles on which the country was founded, applying Christianity dynamically to present day problems. Born into a poor-white Tennessee sharecropper family he became a preacher of the gospel. Deprived of his church, jailed, beaten, he was not silenced. Unprejudiced, he looked upon black and white alike.

223. The Economic Future of the Caribbean, ed. by E. Franklin Frazier and Eric Williams. Washington, D.C.: Howard Univ. Press, 1944. 29 (1944): 486-87.

In a historical conference blacks have proclaimed to the world what they think of their plight and what ought to be done about it. The Caribbean countries, having been exploited for the benefit of the controlling nation, will never be economically sound until such control is broken and they can diversify their crops. If colonialism can be destroyed, advocates propose that the islands organize as a federation. But what hope for this when Great Britain is emerging from this war as the greatest power on earth?

224. An Experiment in Modifying Attitudes Toward the Negro, by F. Treadwell Smith. New York: Bureau of Publications, Teachers College, Columbia Univ. 29 (1944): 492-93.

Although Woodson says there is little in this study to interest a scientifically trained historian he discusses it at length, first to show that the author's summary of what has been done to change attitudes is inadequate; and then to show that the experiment was not really significant because so few subjects were tested and there was no adequate control. Woodson discusses the evils of segregation and race prejudice and says that the book's worth is that it shows the need for change.

225. Tuskegee Institute and the Black Belt: A Portrait of a Race, by Annie Kendrick Walker. Richmond, Va.: Dietz Press, 1944. 30 (1945): 87-88.

The author believes that blacks should receive more than they have until now, but that they are not ready to become citizens. Maybe someday! She plays up Tuskegee because of its conservative program. But, Woodson says, the school has taught its students to think and they have read progressive newspapers and magazines. Booker T. Washington was not a conservative. His five finger philosophy in his Atlanta speech was misinterpreted and applied by the segregationists. Woodson ends this review with a tribute of praise to Booker T. Washington.

226. The Negro in American Life, by John Becker. Intro. by Lillian Smith. New York: Julian Messner, 1944.
227. Meet the Negro: A Positive Picture of "America's Tenth Man", by Karl E. Downs. Intro. by E. Stanley Jones. Pasadena, Ca.: The Login Press, 1944. 30 (1945): 89-90.

These publications are a conglomeration of half-baked ideas mixing the meritorious and the questionable, and making no judgments as to cause and effect. The authors are undependable in their facts and standards, and place their emphasis equally on the important and the unimportant.

228. Capitalism and Slavery, by Eric Williams. Chapel Hill, N.C.: The Univ. of North Carolina Press, 1944. 30 (1945): 93-95.

"All the important archives of the British Empire yielded materials" for this essay on slavery from an international point of view, scientifically presented by an able scholar. Dealing with slavery in its commercial and industrial ramifications in the British Empire, the study could equally apply to other European nations. Slavery was the means by which commercial capitalism developed the wealth of Europe in the 18th century, thus creating industrial capitalism in the 19th century, followed by universal revolution. Woodson employs a third of this review to excoriate the British Empire, a democracy of privileged interests, not one of individuals, grabbing the land of weaker nations and controlling their raw materials.

229. La Fondation de la République d'Haïti par Alexandre Pétion, by Dr. François Dalencour. The author, 3 Rue Saint-Cyr, Port-Au-Prince, Haiti, 1944. 30 (1945): 95-97.

Pétion established the Republic of Haiti in 1806 though democracy did not reach to all the people and government was in the hands of the upper class. Written by a Haitian this volume shows Haiti from a viewpoint not usually available to foreigners. The work is chiefly from secondary sources, however; a more fully documented treatment is desirable. Woodson asks to what extent have such documents been preserved. He hopes that from Haitian youths will come historians who will tell an objective and scientific story of Haiti.

230. The Haitian-American Anthology: Haitian Readings from American Authors, by Mercer Cook and Dantes Bellegarde. Port-Au-prince, Haïti: Imprimerie de l'État, 1944. 30 (1945): 97-99.

Dr. Cook, on leave in Haiti, as Supervisor of the English-Teaching Project, in collaboration with Dantes Bellegarde, compiled this anthology for the use of his students. The work was not published for sale. The selections are chiefly comments of North Americans on Haiti, presented under five headings: history, life and customs, nature, art, and folklore. The volume could profitably be used in schools elsewhere engaged in the study of Haiti.

231. Panorama de la Musica Afroamericana, by Newtor R. Ortiz Oderigo. Buenos Aires, Argentina: Editorial Claridad, 1944. 30 (1945): 99-100.

The author describes in Spanish the development of black music in the United States: work songs, spirituals, blues, minstrelsy, ragtime and jazz. The book will help to convince Latin Americans that North American blacks have made a distinct contribution to culture and will expose the propaganda falsely attributing such music to whites. Pictures and biographical information are borrowed extensively from Maud Cuney-Hare's work without giving due credit. Woodson, commenting on what the book does not do, asks a number of questions which the author might have profitably developed.

232.   Without Bitterness: Western Nations in Post-War Africa, by A.A. Nwafor Orizu. New York: Creative Age Press, 1944.   30 (1945): 100-102.

After the Berlin Conference of 1885, Europeans decided to take over Africa and exploit the natives, a method of economic imperialism. But as some natives acquired education and modernization they resented and questioned the repression under which so many were held. They united in demanding change. The author of this volume advocates the aggressive policy of Nnamdi. Azikiwe rather than the conservative course of J.E.K. Aggrey. The author dwells more on the history of Nigeria than of other parts. If the conquerer will not move out peacefully, Orizu advocates revolution.

233.   The Rising Wind, by Walter F. White. New York: Doubleday, Doran and Co., 1945.   30 (1945): 223-25.

Walter White visited the front to observe the condition and treatment of black soldiers. The book reports chiefly what has already been told in the press, but performs a service by organizing the information in one volume from which conclusions can be drawn. The author recommended to General Eisenhower the brigading of soldiers of both races, and officers have also urged mixed units. The rising wind is a warning of trouble if a change does not come in the military and at home.

234. The Negro Artist Comes of Age. A National Survey of Contemporary American Artists. Foreward by John Davis Hatch, Jr. Intro., "Up Till Now," by Alain Locke. Albany, N.Y.: Albany Institute of History and Art, 1945.   30 (1945): 227-28.

An exhibit at the Albany Institute of History and Art shows that black artists are making an esthetic contribution equal to "the greater body of creative artists in our country." The Institute has found 41 deserving of notice, and regrets that only 12 are listed in Who's Who in American Art. Alain Locke's introduction says in concise form what he has said in expanded form in his other works. Should this group be set off by itself as black artists, or exhibited with others and considered as artists who happen to be black? In past experience Henry O. Tanner and others who achieved distinction found they had first to be known and supported by their fellow blacks.

235. Unsung Americans Sung, ed. by W.C. Handy. New York: Handy Brothers Music Co., 1944. 30 (1945): 228-30.

Handy has edited a book of songs to famous blacks in history. Some of the verses have been written by Langston Hughes, Alain Locke, and George W. Schuyler, but the overall effect is very uneven, and Woodson says the rest of the poetry does not rise to the level of the music. He complains of the bogus picture of Crispus Attucks and the inclusion of the "infamous" with the famous. Yet he considers the book a "commendable undertaking" which shows that the race is now conscious of the heroism of the noble men and women who have led it thus far out of the wilderness.

236. Frederick Douglass: Selections from his Writings, ed. with an intro. by Philip S. Foner. New York: International Publishers, 1945. 30 (1945): 230-32.

By far the best short treatment of Douglass, the book amounts to a biography which reveals the stature of this leader whom the editor ranks above Wendell Phillips and William Lloyd Garrison, and his relations with the abolitionists in this country and abroad, and with other important contemporaries. Woodson's review contrasts Douglass's philosophy with that of the Garrisonians and he predicts that Douglass will be crowned by history as one of the greatest statesmen of his time and a far-sighted humanitarian.

237. The Role of the Supreme Court in American Government and Politics, by Charles Groves Haines. Berkeley, Ca.: Univ. of California Press, 1944. 30 (1945): 232-34.

The author considers that historians have paid undue attention to Federalist views even after the downfall of that party, and their attention should now be directed to the States' Rights-Republican views. Woodson says the author's theory sounds impressive but analyzed loses weight. The author, he says, misuses the word democracy; the States' Rights party impeded rather than promoted democracy. Woodson uses the rest of the review to prove this point.

238. The United States, 1865-1900: A Survey of Current Literature with Abstracts of Unpublished Dissertations, ed. by Curtis Wiswell Garrison. Fremont, Oh.: The Rutherford B. Hayes and the Lucy Webb Hayes Foundation, 1944. 30 (1945): 234-35.

The volume is a classified digest of historical literature published between September 1942 and September 1943 treating of Rutherford B. Hayes and measures he promoted. The work also includes abstracts of unpublished dissertations relating to American history accepted during that year. Woodson praises the classified arrangement as timesaving for the student but is highly critical of the omission of works relating to blacks. Only a few were included. He absolves Dr. Wesley who is listed among the editors from blame, because his great responsibilities otherwise would leave him little time for details of this volume.

239. The Encyclopedia of the Negro. Preparatory volume with reference lists and reports, ed. by W.E.B. DuBois and Guy B. Johnson and prepared with the cooperation of E. Irene Diggs, Agnes C.I. Donohugh, Guion Johnson, Rayford W. Logan and L.D. Reddick. Intro. by Anson Phelps Stokes. New York: The Phelps-Stokes Fund, 1945. 30 (1945): 339-42.

After strongly advocating the need for an encyclopedia of the Negro, Woodson says that for thirty years there has been talk of such a work that amounted only to talk. The editors of this proposed encyclopedia have brought out this volume to show the public what they intend to do. Instead of that they should have proceeded with the task. Anson Phelps Stokes could easily finance the venture. But they should not expect the black race to finance what is being produced by the other race. Dr. DuBois is a very old man, and Guy B. Johnson's former books have "set forth mainly what the race has not rather than what it has done."

240. Color and Democracy: Colonies and Peace, by W.E.B. DuBois. New York: Harcourt, Brace and Co., 1945. 30 (1945): 342-43.

International conferences of nations combatting the Axis powers have been planning the reconstruction of the world, raising hopes among races previously deprived for a plan to redress their grievances. To bring these complaints before the representatives, blacks in Africa, America and the West Indies have resorted to the press and publication of books and pamphlets presenting their demands. In this appeal for democracy for all men Dr. DuBois is mindful that Great Britain is determined to maintain the empire as heretofore and he warns of the danger of it.

241. Experiments in Democracy, by USO Divisions of the National Board YWCA. New York: National Board of the YWCA, 1945. 30 (1945): 344-45.

Woodson makes his review of this book a condemnation of the kind of Christianity which advocates and practices jimcrow. The democracy advocated in this book is a qualified democracy, but, says Woodson, it is an advance beyond that usually practiced by the YWCA. The Church and this organization should disestablish themselves as jimcrowing agencies and reorganize on the principles taught by the Great Nazarene.

242. <u>For a New Africa</u>. Proceedings of the Conference on Africa held in New York City on April 14, 1945, together with addresses by Max Yergan and Paul Robeson. New York: Council on African Affairs, 1945. 30 (1945): 346-48.

The Conference, organized by Max Yergan after his stay in Africa, to disseminate accurate information about that continent, is in its seventh year. After a long identification of Max Yergan and of Paul Robeson and praise for his wife, Woodson declares that the African's share in the victory of the war must be the removal of the evils inflicted by their European conquerors. The Conference wants to see established an international authority for colonial affairs, the development of Africa, and its liberation.

243. <u>Inching Along: An Autobiographical Story</u>, by Henry Damon Davidson. Nashville: National Publication Co., 1944. 30 (1945): 443-44.

The author gives an account of his life and the work that he did in founding the Centerville Industrial Institute, now the Bibb County Training School, Centerville, Alabama. At times he stresses things not of great importance and indulges in self-adulation. Nevertheless, the book is of value to historians as an account touching on his contemporaries: Dr. James H. Dillard, Booker T. Washington, and H. Council Trenholm, local judges and the governor of the state.

244. <u>The Virgin Islands and their People</u>, by J. Antonio Jarvis. Philadelphia, Pa.: Dorrance and Co., 1945. 30 (1945): 444-45.

The author, a native of the Islands and a teacher at Charlotte Amalie, studied in the U. S.. He refers to the ancient landmarks of the Islands established under Danish control, and describes climate, plants, animals and fisheries. He presents the Islands as part of a general view of the Caribbean area and describes the race admixture of the people who deserve a higher rating than to be referred to as poor and neglected. They have both suffered and prospered under American rule, and the author sees hope of the growth of democracy.

245. <u>African Journey</u>, by Eslanda Goode Robeson. New York: The John Day Co., 1945. 30 (1945): 445-46.

Mrs. Robeson's diary tells of her visit to the West Coast of Africa chiefly touching the ports. The public should be grateful for these observations. Others who have made the journey should leave accounts as the public needs additional comment on present conditions on this continent. The authorities do not allow visitors to penetrate the interior unless they are sympathizers with the "economic imperialists" but even a casual visitor learns something nevertheless.

246. The Congo, by John LaTouche and Andre Cauvin. New York: Willow White and Co., 1945. 30 (1945): 446-47.

Written in a readable style the book tells of the conquest and administration of the Congo, evidently to show what Belgium has done for this colony. In his review Woodson supplies the unfavorable aspects which the authors omit: Stanley's use of the Congo as a pawn, Leopold's tricky seizure of the area, and his atrocities, and the error of the United States in recognizing the Congo Free State and thus giving it international standing. The authors make excuses and tell of improvements such as better schools and medical services.

247. Build Together Americans, by Rachel Davis DuBois. New York, Philadelphia: Hinds, Hayden and Eldridge, 1945. 30 (1945): 447-49.

Woodson highly praises this book which deals with the author's experiences in intercultural education. She discusses American culture and such subjects as prejudice, social psychology, and wounded personalities. Woodson says the race-hating class advance arguments for continuing race-hate, as each race desires to remain what it is. Understood and assimilated, differences could enrich our culture with significant contributions to make the United States outstanding among the nations of the world.

248. Lincoln the President, by J.G. Randall. Two volumes. New York: Dodd, Mead and Co., 1945. 31 (1946): 107-111.

This long review expresses Woodson's differences with the author who aroused his ire at the outset by stating that Stephen A. Douglass was right and Lincoln wrong on squatter sovereignty. His attitude on slavery drew from Woodson the label "a medievalist dabbling with modern problems." The author thinks the Civil War was not inevitable but could have been settled amicably. He blames McClellan's failure on interference by cliques, and considers the abolitionists fanatics. Woodson refutes each point at length. The volume is an account of the Civil War with Lincoln as the chief actor. The author sits in judgment on the dead and hears one side of the case at the expense of the other for which he has unconcealed antipathy. This is history made to order.

249. A Nation of Nations, by Louis Adamic. New York: Harper and Brothers, 1945. 31 (1946): 111-13.

Though the institutions of the United States are of

Anglo-Saxon origin, the people who have built upon
them have come from many nations to make a very
different civilization here. This country is not
another England. With the exception of language and
literature there are few similarities between the two
countries. All of the elements have made a
contribution and are still shaping our destiny,
including the blacks, whom the author does not
ignore. Woodson points out, however, that some errors
have been made in identifications and some important
people have not been mentioned.

250. Black Metropolis: A Study of Negro Life in a Northern
City, by St. Clair Drake and Horace R. Cayton. New York:
Harcourt Brace and Co., 1945. 31 (1946): 113-16.

After narrating the city's historical background, the
book deals with what Chicago is today as a result of
black migration and the formation of a Black Belt.
The authors discuss color line, job ceiling,
democracy, economics and politics, showing their
inter-relationships with other parts of the city.
Woodson wishes someone would translate the book's
"highly professional language", familiar only to the
new social scientists, into English understandable by
the Average American.

251. Lay My Burden Down, ed. by B.A. Botkin. Chicago: The
Univ. of Chicago Press, 1945. 31 (1946): 119-21.

The Federal Writers' Project made possible the
publication of this book, a folk history of slavery, a
collection of narratives many obtained orally. The
editor included many which documented the benevolent
treatment of slaves by kind masters which induced
Woodson to ask if the editor were pro-slavery. From
the mass of 10,000 narratives collected by the Federal
Writers' Project out of which these were chosen,
another editor could tell quite a different story.
The most interesting part of the book is that devoted
to tall tales, and Woodson points out their African
origin which the editor failed to do. In spite of its
defects this is a valuable work.

252. The Senate and the Versailles Mandate System, by
Rayford W. Logan. Washington, D.C.: The Minorities
Publishers, 1945. 31 (1946): 121-23.

According to the Covenant of the League of Nations, by
the Mandate System peoples who because of the war
ceased to be under the sovreignty of states formerly
governing them would be under control of the League of
Nations. Through the conflicting attitudes of the
U.S. Senate, this treaty was rejected. Dr. Logan ably
reports the debates of the 64th and 65th Congresses,
and gives detailed accounts of positions taken by the

leaders.   This is useful background for the 1945
situation when the Senate must consider Trusteeship
(Mandate System) of dependent nations adopted by the
U.N. Conference in San Francisco.   In predicting that
hostility in the Senate will continue, the author goes
beyond the bounds of the historian.   Woodson says our
 statesmen   refuse to learn from experience and ignore
the verdict of the past.

253. Brazil, An Interpretation, by Gilberto Freyre.   New
York: Alfred A. Knopf, 1945.   31 (1946): 123-25.

Freyre, in these lectures delivered at the University
of Indiana in 1944 presents an interpretation   of
Brazil based on historical background.   The Portuguese
conflicted with the Indians and brought in slaves from
Africa,   adding   another   culture   to   the
Spanish-Portuguese-Indian.   But the absence of hard
social gradations made it possible for anyone with
qualifications   to rise to the highest prominence.
Brazil has attained a unique position through its
political economy.   "Only   Soviet   Russia   may   be
compared with Brazil.   These two countries are shining
examples of what the policy of equality and justice
for all will do in the transformation of a nation."

254.   Thenceforward and Forever Free, by Bess V. Ehrmann.
New York: Horizon House, 1945.   31 (1946): 227-29.

After Emancipation some blacks crossed the Ohio River
into Rockport, Indiana, inspired to be living in the
same part of the country as Lincoln.   Ms.   Ehrmann
tells stories about some of them.   Mary Lee's mother
left her as a child in the care of Aunt Lefie, a white
woman concerned about the unattended children of black
working mothers.   Besides watching the children, she
began teaching them and so developed a day nursery.
Albert Merritt, a young black, telling stories to idle
neglected white boys, organized The Junior Club at his
own expense.   These and other stories show what good
can result from cooperation.

255.   Race and Democratic Society, by Franz Boas. New York:
J.J. Augustin, Publisher, 1945.   31 (1946): 231-32.

This collection of writings by a great scientist,
among the first in this country to disprove   the
prevailing theories of race and to show how acquired
cultural   habits   are   mistaken   for   hereditary
characteristics, discusses Jews and Aryans and various
aspects of the black's past.   He makes an appeal to
Americans to get rid of prejudice and antipathies and
work for a united future and an international state
based on democracy.   There must be freedom of teaching
to advance these principles.

256. Problemas Sociales y Económicos de México, by joint authorship. Mexico City, Mexico: Edición de la Secretaria del Trabajo y Prévisión Social, 1945. 31 (1946): 232-33.

Fundamental to the reforms promoted by the collaborators on this volume is the purchasing power of the worker's wages. They discuss the price of silver, agricultural settlements, unemployment, hygiene and medicine, industrial and social conditions. To achieve in any of these areas there must be improvement in education and equality among all men. This book is eloquent evidence of the fact that these principles of social reform are deeply rooted in Mexico.

257. Come Out Fighting, by Trezzvant W. Anderson. Teisendorf: Salzburger Druckerei und Verlag, 1945. 31 (1946): 233-35.

This book gives credit to black soldiers of the 761st Tank Battalion for their achievements in World War II. It pays tribute to the men who died in action, with brief biographical sketches of the most outstanding. The author discusses the actual fighting in "Into the Bulge," "Cracking the Siegfried Line," and other such topics. The book is written in newspaper style which makes it very readable. Published especially for members of the battalion it deserves wider distribution.

258. The Negro and the Post War World: A Primer, by Rayford W. Logan. Washington, D.C.: The Minorities Publishers, 1945. 31 (1946): 235-36.

At the close of World War II, authorities thought the pattern of segregation would persist, but Dr. Logan undertakes to show that the old policy will no longer work. He has said much in too concentrated a form, difficult for the average reader to digest, but those with more informed backgrounds may become convinced that the black is both a national and an international factor. In the planning for universal peace and the post-war reconstruction, he must be taken into consideration.

259. Africa Advancing: A Study of Rural Education and Agriculture in West Africa and the Belgian Congo, by Jackson Davis, Thomas M. Campbell and Margaret Wrong. New York: Friendship Press, 1945. 31 (1946): 238-39.

This is the usual missionary effort, the authors of which spent only six months among the people, and it takes in only seven countries of Africa. Natives do not readily give information to foreigners, but in self-defence tell them the reverse of the truth, Woodson says. The book's chief value lies in the commentaries on the changes occurring and those that must follow the San Francisco charter. Education of all the people is the first essential. They will make new teachers and the new teachers will make a new civilization.

260. The Foxes of Harrow, by Frank Yerby. New York: The Dial Press, 1946. 31 (1946): 353-54.

This historical novel is an all but perfect portrayal of New Orleans in the ante-bellum scene of Louisiana. The story of Stephen Fox and the plantation called Harrow brings in the characters of Desiree, the octoroon, the Negro Inch who could never accept slavery, the Acadians, and the Free People of Color. The slavery debate reaches Harrow as does the news of John Brown's raid. While referring to the novel as "great", Woodson suggests ways in which it could be improved.

261. Negro Labor, A National Problem, by Robert C. Weaver. New York: Harcourt, Brace and Co., 1946. 31 (1946): 354-57.

A brief history of the black worker includes the policies and "methods of evasion and subterfuge" impeding the orders to make full use of labor supply for speeding the war effort. Even after the executive order prohibiting discrimination in war plants the U.S. Employment Service and the U.S. Department of Education were slow in changing their attitudes. This is a timely and valuable book which could have been improved in style, and whose language could have been simplified to reach the average worker, though it is a contribution for the economist.

262. Lincoln and the South, by J.G. Randall. Baton Rouge, La.: The Univ. of Louisiana Press, 1946. 31 (1946): 357-60.

Dr. Randall delivered these four lectures at Louisiana State University which published them as a volume. His bias affects his interpretation of facts as in his attempt to show Lincoln "sympathetic towards the South because he was born in the South, married a Southern woman and was a Jeffersonian liberal." Randall's reasoning is puerile. Some of this may be mere flattery to please his public. The rest of the review is Woodson's essay on Lincoln's true sympathy with the South, his efforts to avoid the war, to secure gradual and compensated emancipation and to transplant freedmen to foreign soil. In 1862, discovering that the colonization plan did not work, he warned the secessionists that he would emancipate the slaves. Lincoln shifted toward radicalism from year to year.

263. Essays in the History of the American Negro, by Herbert Aptheker. New York: International Publishers, 1945.   31 (1946): 360-62.

Aptheker's thesis, that slaves were not satisfied with their lot and kept up a day to day resistance to slavery is heartily supported by Woodson in this review. Proslavery defenders have advanced the propaganda that slavery was a benevolent institution. Even the American Historical Review attacked Aptheker's use of terms such as "slavocrats" and "lords of the lash", as well as the number of blacks who died in the Civil War, the number verified by the United States Adjutant General.

264. Florida under Five Flags, by Rembert W. Patrick. Gainesville, Fla.: Univ. of Florida Press, 1945.   31 (1946): 362-64.

While praising the production of this interesting volume Woodson points out in detail the author's omission of the mention of blacks in the period of exploration and other historical periods. For example, he neglects to tell of the welcome given by the Spaniards to escaping slaves or the close relation between blacks and Indians. The author relates the educational progress of blacks in recent times and publishes statistics to show that funds spent for their schools fall far below those alloted to white schools.

265. Brotherhood of Sleeping Car Porters, by Brailsford R. Brazeal. New York: Harper and Brothers, 1946.   31 (1946): 364-67.

"An important chapter" in black history, this volume is required reading for all those interested in labor problems. The story of the Brotherhood, founded in 1925, depicts the struggles of A. Philip Randolph to obtain relief for these railroad workers from long hours, small wages, and rejection by unions. The Pullman Company "assumed the attitude of philanthropy" as there was never any shortage of workers. Through Randolph's efforts the Pullman company finally had to recognize the Brotherhood as the properly qualified bargaining agency.

266. El Engano de las Razas, by Fernando Ortiz. La Habana, Cuba: Arrow Press, 1946.   31 (1946): 371-73.

The concept of race is dangerous--there is only one race: the human race. The author discusses the leading theories of race and exposes efforts toward rationalization by racists. The widespread myth of race advanced by the Nazis has not yet been dispelled and agents of hate are still actively promoting

insidious   racism.   The   book   shows   the   need   for
scientific study of the social order.

267. Race Attitudes and Education, Hoernle Memorial
Lecture, 1946, by E.G. Malherbe, Principal, Natal Univ.
Johannesburg, S. Africa: South African Institute of Race
Relations, 1946.   31 (1946): 485-88.

This brief volume was prepared to enlighten soldiers
from South Africa going to the front.   The Director
had   the   men   in   the   armed   forces   fill   out   a
questionnaire to find out what they thought about
those commonly referred to in South Africa as
Non-Europeans.   Discovering   their   prejudices,   the
Director   could   then   dispel   doubts   and   fears.   The
author believes that education will help the natives
to   understand   the   problems   of   the   Europeans,   but
Woodson says: "If they are trained as have been the
Negroes   of   the   United   States, who have been the
victims   of   Negro   education   rather   than   thinkers
produced by the education of the Negro, such natives
will be toadies and cowards like the thousands of this
type of mis-educated Negroes in the United States."

268.   Holders   of   Doctorates   among   Negroes,   by   Harry
Washington Greene.   Boston: Meador Publishing Co., 1946.
31 (1946): 488-91.

The chief value of this book lies in its listing of
blacks with Ph.D.'s and the positions they presently
hold.   However,   there   is   a great deal of repetition,
and misinformation.   No   distinction   is   made   between
valid graduate schools and "diploma mills" so there is
confusion with pseudo-Ph.D's. Many of these persons,
trained in the North, have not learned to think, have
accepted a biased view of slavery (benevolent) and
blacks (no history) and only know how to do what they
are told to do by white people.

269.   La Poblacion Negra de Mexico, 1510-1810, Estudio
Etnohistorico,   by   Gonzalo   Aguirre   Beltran.   Mexico:
Ediciones Fuente Cultural, 1946.   31 (1946): 491-94.

The author has begun the tremendous task of uncovering
the racial origins of Mexico.   He searches out the
tribal origins of blacks imported in the slave trade
and faces the difficulty of trying to identify names
of tribes in the confusion of those assigned by
writers who labeled them in their own ways. He gives
statistics relating to the admixture of three elements
in Mexican population: Portuguese, Indian, and black.
This scientifically prepared study will be influential
among scholars in America and Europe.

270.   Annuario Estatistico do Brasil, Ano VI, 1941-1945, by
Instituto Brasileiro de Geografia E. Estatistica, Conselho

Nacional de Estatistica. Rio de Janeiro, Brazil: Servico Grafico de Instituto Brasileiro de Geografia E. Estatistico, 1946. 32 (1947): 124-26.

Persons interested in Brazil will find this volume a valuable source of information. While it compiles the facts usually given by official publications, there are no statistics earmarked as racial since no color line exists in Brazil. A large amount of space is devoted to education.

271. Annuario de Estudios Americanos, Vol. I, 1944; Vol. II, 1945, by the Escuela de Estudios Hispano-Americanos de la Universidad de Sevilla. Sevilla, Spain: Talleres tipograficos de Editorial Catolica Espanola. 32 (1947): 126-27.

These are the first two volumes of annuals to document the participation of Spain in the Europeanization of America and Africa, by a school of Hispanic American studies. The treatments in these two volumes emphasize "discovery, exploration and colonization to the credit of the Spaniards themselves" rather than the movements in general and all the participants; and sources used are entirely Spanish or Latin. There are other records, and in future volumes there may be wider documentation as expected by modern historiography.

272. Amber Gold, by A.H. Maloney. Boston: Meador Publishing Co., 1946. 32 (1947): 127-28.

This autobiography of a man little known is valuable as a document showing the adjustment of a native of Trinidad to the situations he meets in a very different environment. His experiences take him to Lincoln University, Columbia, General Theological Seminary, and other places to teach at several colleges, and finally at Howard. The book is a contribution to the history of West Indian immigrants to the United States and the fine record of their achievements.

273. Grown-up Liberia, by Francis Mitchell. New York: The Author. 32 (1947): 128-30.

The author, a native of Trinidad who settled in West Africa to do medical research, has a much higher opinion of the natives of the country than of the government, which he excoriates. The lives of the Americo-Liberians are based on selfishness. In their cowardice and greediness they are incapable of dealing with foreigners and are hostile to them. World War II has brought changes which may improve things, but the author is not very optimistic.

274.   The Future of South-West Africa, by J.D. Rheinallt
Jones. Johannesburg, S. Africa: South African Institute of
Race Relations, 1946.   32 (1947): 130-31.

This booklet presents the effort of General Smuts to
obtain the permission of the United Nations for the
integration of South-West Africa, Bechuanaland,
Basutoland and Swaziland into the Union of South
Africa. The author, discussing the Mandates worked
out in the Treaty of Paris 1919, shows that this
system was not successful. Reports in this booklet
show that the status of the natives in the Union of
South Africa "stands out as a menacing terror to those
natives in the protectorates." They fear that
integration may mean the same degraded status for them.

275.   American Sea Power since 1775, by members of the
Departments of English, History, and Government of the
United States Naval Academy, J. Roger Fredland, William W.
Jeffries, Neville T. Kirk, Thomas F. McManus, Elmer B.
Potter, Richard S. West, and Allan Westcott. Philadelphia:
J.B. Lippincott Co., 1947.   32 (1947): 232-34.

The authors have presented valuable information on the
history of the Navy, devoting most space to recent
developments, not by gripping narratives but by
technological advances. While the volume is not
thoroughly documented, it is on a high level. They
have written without reference to the racial
composition of the Navy as history should be written.
But blacks want it made clear that "in proportion to
the population of their race in this country they have
supplied a larger number of men than any other element
in the United States." Rehearsing this story is one
way to combat race hate and the inequity it produces.

276. Why Men Hate, by Samuel Tennenbaum. New York: The
Beechurst Press, 1947.   32 (1947): 244-45.

Only by uprooting hate will men save the world from
destruction and self-extermination. More and more
thinkers are arriving at this conclusion. This volume
develops the concept of the human race as a unity.
The author uses psychology and sociology to interpret
history by showing how the bigot, with his distorted
personality, uses hate as an escape from reality, and
demagogues and opportunists use bigotry for their
selfish ends. He draws upon the history of the Negro
in relations with Europe and America to make his views
clear and gives instances of mob violence towards
Mexicans, Japanese, Jews and other victims of bigotry.

277.   Jim Crow America, by Earl Conrad. New York: Duel,
Sloan and Pearce, 147 [sic].   32 (1947): 245-47.

Both a history and an account of personal experiences

by "the only white man employed in regular full-time capacity as a bureau manager and columnist by the black press" the volume starts with the author's investigation of an unpunished rape in Alabama. It deals with restrictive covenants, prejudiced newspapers and prejudiced historians, exposing "progaganda which masquerades as learning," and explodes many other theories justifying discrimination.

278. Trinidad Village, by Melville J. Herskovits and Frances S. Herskovits. New York: Alfred A. Knopf, 1947. 32 (1947): 247-49.

A stimulating work, the book nevertheless does not give sufficient background but provides a foundation for others to build upon. The authors found something new: a Protestant black culture in the Caribbean, in the settlement Toco. Life here resembled "almost any Negro community in our own rural South." They saw traces of African worship in religious practices, resulting in a hybrid cult. Other elements of the social order in Toco receive treatment.

279. Shining Trumpets, A History of Jazz, by Rudi Blesh. New York: Alfred A. Knopf, 1947. 32 (1947): 249-50.

Shining Trumpets is a more comprehensive work than the author's previous production, This is Jazz. In attempting to define jazz, the author is on controversial ground, raising questions on which musicians will not be able to agree. He deals successfully with the African origins of this music, its tentative beginnings in New Orleans and the "sociological implications of the course which the development of jazz has taken in modern times."

280. Liberia: A Century of Survival, 1847-1947, by Raymond Leslie Buell. Philadelphia: Univ. of Pennsylvania Press, 1947. 32 (1947): 252-54.

The blacks who settled Liberia and their descendants took as their models their former proslavery masters. Thus the Americo-Liberians exploited the natives and the government neglected the hostile tribes and the hinterland. The United States has done little to help Liberia. The Administration, though opposed by Congress, encouraged Firestone's occupancy of a million acres for rubber production. The use of the country as a United States naval base may be to Liberia's advantage. The author deplores the country's lack of sanitation as well as the one-party system, and urges the establishment of a representative agency to administer affairs. A book worth reading.

281. Kingsblood Royal, by Sinclair Lewis. New York: Random House, Inc., 1947. 32 (1947): 364-66.

This historical novel is unique in that a well-recognized author has portrayed "race prejudice in such style as to arouse nation-wide interest." Appearing just about a century after <u>Uncle Tom's Cabin</u>, it may have the same potentialities. The Protagonist's world changes overnight when in reply to a speech insulting to blacks he impulsively tells his friends he has recently discovered that he is 1/32 black himself. Woodson comments that passing for white is a common practice, though John Hope and H.A. Hunt, apparently Caucasian, chose not to do so.

282. <u>Wilson, The Road to the White House</u>, by Arthur S. Link. Princeton, N.J.: Princeton Univ. Press, 1947. 32 (1947): 366-69.

Dr. Link has used all the facts that available documents can supply in a narrative as gripping as a novel. The book presents Wilson's life prior to his induction as President. Treating of the participation of blacks in the election of 1912, Link goes thoroughly into Wilson's vascillating policy as he tries to please all factions and finally, with the split in the Republican party, realizes that securing the support of blacks is no longer a political expediency.

283. <u>New Day Ascending</u>, by Fred L. Brownlee. Boston: The Pilgrim Press, 1946. 32 (1947): 369-71.

An important chapter in the history of education for blacks since the Civil War, the work deals with the American Missionary Association, the institutions this agency assisted, and men like George Whipple, Charles Hall, and John G. Fee who sacrificed their lives to activate the program. Woodson says the spirit of the missionary has gone. Some positions in black schools are going to southern whites who "have not been able to abandon segregation, and their Negro coworkers choose the role of Uncle Toms to feather their own nests."

284. <u>Into the Main Stream, A Survey of Best Practices in Race Relations</u>, by Charles S. Johnson and Associates, Elizabeth L. Allen, Horace M. Bond, Margaret McCullough and Alma Forrest Polk. Chapel Hill, N.C.: Univ. of North Carolina Press, 1947. 32 (1947): 371-73.

Advancement is possible even in the land of peonists and mobocrats. These professionals avoid a discussion of difficult questions. There is not much new in this report. They suggest the stimulation of agencies now in operation. The YMCA and the YWCA in the ample time they have had "have been unable to change the attitude of the so-called Christian people." Though there is an absence of achievement among "self-styled inter-racial committees" even mere talk will do some good.

285. Education for Negroes in Mississippi since 1910, by Charles H. Wilson, Sr. Boston: Meador Publishing Co., 1947. 32 (1947): 374-75.

In a compilation of data containing a miscellany of information, Mr. Wilson reports only favorable things rather than the failure of the state in educating blacks, though he publishes figures showing how much less black teachers are paid than white teachers. The system in Mississippi, where demagogues insist that blacks should not be educated at public expense is far from the status of a progressive southern state like North Carolina. The compiler "shows much enthusiasm for his task, but he is not always accurate." The volume will serve as a guide to documentary materials for further research.

286. Os Pretos Norte Americanos, A Treatment of the Spiritual Progress of the North American Negro, by Francisco Faria Netto. São Paulo, Brazil: Livraria Liberdade, Rue da liberdade, 659, 1946. 32 (1947): 382-84.

The Brazilian author gives a rather blurred account of the background of North American blacks before going into efforts for their enlightenment. His knowledge of the Churches is limited, and there are omissions in his list of accomplished blacks as well as institutions of learning. Nevertheless, since few books concerning North American blacks have appeared in Brazil this is a useful work which will arouse interest in the subject and lead to further research.

287. The Walls Came Tumbling Down, by Mary White Ovington. New York: Harcourt, Brace and Co., 1947. 32 (1947): 501-503.

This study by a white founder of NAACP first discusses conditions in both the North and the South. Following the Civil War the work of the abolitionists was practically undone. "If the United States was to be maintained on a plane higher than peonage and serfdom enforced by rope and fagot, the thinking classes had to take immediate action to preserve what little civilization the nation had achieved." Miss Ovington's story is the drama of the earlier years of the NAACP whose dedicated members stirred white consciences, and roused blacks from lethergy to fight for freedom.

288. The Record of American Diplomacy, sel. and ed. by Ruhl J. Barnett. New York: Alfred A. Knopf, 1947. 32 (1947): 503-506.

The compiler of these documents related to the foreign policy of the United States, has selected more than 300 and arranged them chronologically for which he deserves thanks. The volume will be of most use in the classroom. It must be kept in mind that questionable politics and changes of administration make it difficult to determine just what is the foreign policy of the country at times. It is often the will of political bosses rather than the will of the people of the nation.

289. Democracy's Negroes, by Arthur Furr. Boston: The House of Edinboro, 1947. 32 (1947): 509-10.

In this miscellany of data from the black armed forces in World War II the chief ingredient consists of the releases sent out by the War Department. Included are lists of soldiers, their posts, and the engagements in which they figured. "In the unraveling of the threads of history by prying into the mass of source materials ... there will come to light many hidden truths which will put the scientifically trained historian in the position to" evaluate the services of the black soldiers. Texts on social science used in the schools often evaluate the black only as a criminal; hence, the service of this book will be to help set the record straight.

290. Democracy and Empire in the Caribbean, by Paul Blanshard. New York: The Macmillan Co., 1947. 32 (1947): 511-13.

Imperialists have exploited the area and the author makes a case against them as criminals on a high level. He considers clashes inevitable. Federation might have developed better if originated before differing cultural influences took over. Elected legislatures should replace the present colonial governors; but the danger of demagogues must be kept in mind, as well as communism and the undue influences of Russia.

291. The City of Women, by Ruth Landes. New York: The Macmillan Co., 1947. 32 (1947): 513-15.

The author was sent to Bahia to learn how people behave when the blacks among them are not oppressed. She found that though not racially oppressed they suffer from political and economic tyranny. Cut off by poverty from modern institutions they celebrate the candombles in which women play the leading roles. They are the priestesses possessed by special gods; they sacrifice to the Queen of the Sea and stage other rites which stir emotions. The book tells of a country where women are really great.

292. To Secure these Rights. The Report of the President's Committee on Civil Rights. Washington, D.C.: United States Government Printing Office, 1947. 33 (1948): 91-93.

The committee of fifteen members was charged to determine how the government could improve civil rights. The volume reviews the restrictions and outrages inflicted on blacks, and shows how they are also being imposed on other minorities. The committee suggests immediate practical action, beginning with the reorganization of the Civil Rights Section of the Department of Justice, and Civil Rights agencies or commissions in the FBI, Congress, and the Office of the President, and also proposes laws to be enacted to guarantee the freedoms promised in the Constitution.

293. The Negro in Mississippi, 1865-1890, by Vernon Lane Wharton. Ed. with a foreward by A.R. Newsome as one of The James Sprunt Studies in History and Political Science. Chapel Hill, N.C.: The Univ. of North Carolina Press, 1947. 33 (1948): 94-96.

The black vote secured victory for the Republican party which controlled Mississippi for eight years. White supremacists, having overthrown the reconstructionists, resorted to terrorism to silence the blacks. The author has used formerly neglected sources and shown broadmindedness unlike the pseudo-historians, John W. Burgess and W.A. Dunning and the writers influenced by them. When he "abandons the role of the historian and preaches defeatism and social frustration" Woodson takes issue with him.

294. Negro Business and Business Education, by Joseph A. Pierce. A production resulting from the cooperation of Atlanta Univ. and the National Urban League with the assistance of the General Education Board. New York: Harper and Brothers, 1947. 33 (1948): 97-99.

In early days of smaller enterprises blacks in business figured more prominently than in these later days of combinations and large trusts. Infiltration into the business structure will require "a change from the defense philosophy based on race pride" to a realization that success is possible "only by partaking completely of the characteristics of American business." The author lists the disadvantages blacks face and their problems with personnel, and stresses the importance of practical training as well as theoretical education.

295. The Selected Writings of Benjamin Rush, ed. by Dagobert D. Runes. New York: Philosophical Library, 1947. 33 (1948): 101-103.

Benjamin Rush, a medical doctor, advocated changes to

effect a true democracy. He wrote on almost all
topics concerned with the improvement of humanity,
advocated public education, and made early
contributions to penology. Dr. Woodson uses this
review to correct a repeated error: that the article
"A Plan of a Peace Office of the United States," in
Benjamin Banneker's Almanac was written by Banneker.
It was written by his good friend, Dr. Benjamin Rush.

296. The Political and Legislative History of Liberia, by
Charles Henry Huberich. Foreward by Roscoe Pound. Two
volumes. New York: Central Book Co., 1947. 33 (1948):
105-107.

This comprehensive, thorough and authoritative history
of Liberia, published in time for the celebration of
the first century of the Republic, is a detailed
treatment. It begins with the unsuccessful British
effort to colonize the land with free blacks. The
United States, through the American Colonization
Society, was more successful. Lists of agents and
administrators are included and identified, and an
analysis of Liberia's constitution. Huberich also
discusses Americo-Liberians and "pawning", the
government's neglect of the natives, and the sorry
effects of leases and loans.

297. Higher Education for Democracy. A Report of the
President's Commission on Higher Education. Five volumes.
Washington, D.C.: United States Government Printing
Office, 1947. 33 (1948): 234-36.

After listing and identifying 28 members of the
Commission, Woodson summarizes the recommendations in
the five volumes: to double the number of college
students and to heal the breach between those who
educate for work and those who educate for life; free
education through the first two years of college, and
abolition of the quota system and of racial
segregation. The southern commissioners rejected this
last. Woodson says they have not risen above their
medieval constituency and are almost in the same
position where they were when led by John C. Calhoun
and Jefferson Davis.

298. The World's Greatest Hit, by Harry Birdoff. New York:
S.F. Vanni, 1947. 33 (1948): 236-38.

Mrs. Stowe reluctantly granted permission to stage
Uncle Tom's Cabin. In the earliest dramatizations, so
as not to offend certain commercial elements, the
parts of the story depicting the horrors of slavery
were eliminated. Audiences were disappointed and in
future versions the play conformed to the book, in 6
acts, 8 tableaux, and 20 scenes, with immediate
success, depicting an evil so dramatically that

viewers had to repudiate it. Another change occurred: blacks who had taken only comedy parts in the past now played serious roles.

299. <u>All Manner of Men</u>, by Malcolm Ross. New York: Reynal and Hitchcock, 1948. 33(1948): 238-40.

The author points out the inconsistency of the United States making itself a leader in world democracy when, with the South unalterably opposed to equality, we are so lacking in democracy at home. The purpose of the book is to expose this defect in our system and to recommend creation of an agency for guaranteeing equal opportunity for all with powers of enforcement. He calls upon his experience as chairman of the FEPC during World War II and asks cooperation of management, labor, and government and the immediate action of Congress.

300. <u>Francis Lieber, Nineteenth Century Liberal</u>, by Frank Freidel. Baton Rouge, La.: Louisiana State Univ. Press, 1947. 33 (1948): 358-61.

This definitive biography of a German-American describes his European childhood and studies, his escape to England, and arrival in the United States. He became chairman of history and political economy in the University of South Carolina but objected to secession and disliked slavery though supporting only gradual emancipation. He accepted a professorship at Columbia where he remained the rest of his life. He lost the friendship of Charles Sumner because of his dislike of abolitionists, and passed his theories on to Burgess and Dunning, historians who white-washed slave owners.

301. <u>The Story of the Negro</u>, by Arna Bontemps. Illus. by Raymond Lufkin. New York: Alfred A. Knopf, 1948. 33 (1948): 361-63.

The author, "one of the most brilliant and literary men of today," has written a brief account for the general reader, dramatic and moving. "In his charming style [he] has drawn living pictures of the Negro in Africa and abroad." After this glowing praise Woodson points out neglected aspects, omissions in an unbalanced story. However, though the treatment is inadequate and restricted, it will doubtless arouse interest in the subject and lead some to more serious study of black history.

302. <u>The American Churches, An Interpretation</u>, by William Warren Sweet. New York: Abingdon-Cokesbury Press, 1948. 33 (1948): 363-64.

The author endeavors to show that Protestantism, which

had its beginnings about the same time as the discovery of America, developed into two groups, American and European. American Protestantism, affected by the frontier, divided and sub-divided into many sects. Methodist and Baptist churches were totally independent of Europe. The author devotes a chapter to the American black and his religion which leaves many questions unanswered.

303.   Witnesses   for   Freedom,   Negro   Americans   in Autobiography, by Rebecca Chalmers Barton. Foreward by Alain Locke. New York: Harper and Brothers, 1948.   33 (1948): 366-68.

Black people today are in the limelight. Some books are produced to foster hate and repression and others to advance the cause of the oppressed. Some of the latter are written by uninformed persons and "do almost as much harm as good. This work ... belongs to this class." Autobiographies are not necessarily of high literary merit. Many successful people are too modest to write them, while the self-advertising may resort to this method. The compiler has made strange groupings among those included.

304. Zulu Woman, by Rebecca Hourwich Reyher. New York: Columbia Univ. Press, 1948. 33 (1948): 371-72.

The title would quicken a reader's interest, but the author, chiefly a journalist, would not likely produce a serious work of anthropology. Christina, the first wife of Solomon, who had many women, extricated herself from the polygamous relationship. The author's style presents a vivid picture of the social life of the Zulus and attempts to fathom the mind of the African woman and to see the world from her point of view. Woodson resents her unfavorable comparison of their "primitive system" with "so-called civilized people."

305. The American Political Tradition, by Richard Hofstadter. New York: Alfred A. Knopf, 1948. 33 (1948): 479-82.

The author evaluates twelve key characters as shapers of our present political tradition. As an iconoclast he is unsympathetic toward those he presents; but though much of the book is opinion or comment, he supports his theories with fact. Historical persons he judges by today's standards rather than by their own times, while he attempts to evaluate more recent persons too soon for them to be seen in their proper perspective. Woodson faults his passing over William Lloyd Garrison and Frederick Douglass to place greater importance on Wendell Phillips.

306. The Christian Way in Race Relations, by joint authorship, ed. by William Stuart Nelson. New York: Harper and Brothers, 1948. 33 (1948): 482-84.

The Church seems to sit idly by while its members pursue ways the antithesis of its teachings. Intolerance, slavery, economic imperialism are tolerated and the German attitude that whatever is is right. Blacks, however, are endeavoring to bring the Church back to the Apostolic Age when the multitude of them that believed were of one heart and one soul. The contributors to this volume, black churchmen, devotees to the faith of the fathers, are calling upon Christians to square their actions with their words.

307. The Protestant Church and the Negro, by Frank Loescher. New York: Association Press, 1948. 33 (1948): 484-86.

The author's background has supplied information and experience for producing a work of this kind. He reports on what he observed in churches in the North and West, and leaves the South out of the picture (religion there is white supremacy). His findings show the usual restrictions: a few blacks may be acceptable in the back pews; but in case of a large number, they must be segregated in a mission or a separate church. The author finds some hope in the elimination of discrimination at denominational conventions.

308. A Clouded Star, by Anne Parrish. New York: Harper and Brothers, 1948. 33 (1948): 486-88.

A fictionalized account of an incident from the exploits of Harriet Tubman, her rescue of 9 slaves from bondage and their delivery into Canada. The author wisely restricted her narrative to this one feat of Harriet Tubman's, rather than trying to cover her entire life in the book. The account is more fact than fiction. Woodson adds that "as soon as the slaveholders and their descendants can learn to appreciate modern culture and agree to be governed as a democracy" such heroes will be accepted and valued.

309. Education in Haiti, by Mercer Cook. Washington, D.C.: Federal Security Agency, United States Office of Education. 33 (1948): 492-94.

The Haitians had no system of education left them by French colonials, but they adopted the French system until recently. In the American Occupation, agricultural education was introduced as a fundamental necessity, but rejected. When the Occupation ended, the Haitians realized that people in the rural areas could, if prepared, solve the economic problems of the island.   Ninety-two percent of the population are illiterate and only a few speak French.   The disunity wrought by the array of mulattoes against the blacks has led to further exploitation and ignorance.

310.   The Southern Political Scene, 1938-1948,   ed.   by Taylor Cole and John H. Hallowell. Gainesville, Fla.: The Journal of Politics, Univ. of Florida, 1948.   34 (1949): 104-106.

The book comprises reprints from The Journal of Politics, articles by southern professors of political science, writing at a time when the South is in a stage of transition.   They present the reaction of the conservative element to the demand for change, touching on education, conflict with the Federal judiciary, foreign policy, the electorate, states' rights, and other topics.   H.W.   Odum, in the first essay, indicates the difficulty involved in modernization of the South: the deep-rooted situations of traditional southern economy and culture.

311.   Negro Liberation,   by Harry Haygood. New York: International Publishers, 1948.   34 (1949): 106-108.

The author of this book, a black Marxist, while satisfied with constitutional provisions for freedom and equality, deplores the failure of the government to practice the democratic processes.   Segregation, political maneuvers, wage slavery, have defeated the efforts of blacks for economic independence, making them subservient to white capitalists.   "This book advances the idea of peaceful revolution--not the overthrow of any government by force but the democratic administration of the government representative of the masses of those that have not because of the monopoly of those that have."

312.   The Encyclopedia of the African Methodist Episcopal Church. 2nd ed., by R.R. Wright, one of the bishops of the African Methodist Episcopal Church. Philadelphia: The Book Concern of the A.M.E. Church, 1948.   34 (1949): 108-110.

The A.M.E. Church, Woodson says, is the outstanding organization of Negroes in the modern world, and has made important history for 132 years as a force in the uplift of blacks.   Preserving this record is of the greatest importance.   This book should challenge other denominations to preserve their records.   The first edition of this book appeared in 1916 and it has been updated in this volume.   Someone in the next generation "will doubtless be alive to the duty of carrying [it] on" for the sake of the continuity which it deserves.

313. Jazz: A People's Music,   by Sidney Finkelstein.   New York: The Citadel Press, 1948.   34 (1949): 110-12.

Because jazz music developed in the black ghetto in New Orleans, writers have tried to show that this music did not originate with blacks. Today there are many books on jazz, a form of music but recently appreciated. The author is divided in his opinion. He believes that what American music "will finally become depends upon the development of true democracy in America" when the nation appreciates the contribution of all elements of its population. Woodson completes this review by lengthy comment on man's inhumanity to man and the belittlement by whites of the achievements of blacks in Africa and Europe.

314. The United States since 1865. 4th ed., by Louis M. Hacker and Benjamin B. Kendrick with the collaboration of Helene S. Zahler. New York: Appleton-Century-Crofts, 1949. 34 (1949): 222-23.

In this edition the authors have become softer on the captains of industry who supplanted the slaveocracy in control of the federal government. Dr. Hacker sees wealth as the means of saving modern civilization. The authors stress the economic triumph of the nation rather than its moral collapse through anti-Semitism and discrimination. Though blacks are treated with restraint, they show a biased attitude and sympathy for white supremacists. The volume includes also material on the social order and on advances in literature and art.

315. The Story of the Julius Rosenwald Fund, by Edwin R. Embree and Julia Waxman. New York: Harper and Brothers, 1949. 34 (1949): 223-35.

Rosenwald, a philanthropist who with the cooperation of the local populations, established 5,357 school buildings for Negro children in 15 states throughout the rural south, settled $22,000,000 upon the Julius Rosenwald Fund at his death, directing that it be spent within 25 years of his death. A new program brought school construction to an end and concentrated upon such projects as library service, teacher education, and fellowships, and the managers of the fund expended it within 16 years.

316. A Man Called White, by Walter White. New York: The Viking Press, 1948. 34 (1949): 225-27.

The autobiography of one of the most daring and effective men of our times. Though his parents had very little black blood and he appeared white, he chose to identify with blacks. He early learned of the riots and lynchings to which race hate could lead. His work with the local NAACP so impressed its officers that he soon moved to the national office, and, upon the retirement of James Weldon Johnson, became the national Secretary. He could appear unobserved in places inaccessible to known blacks, such as KKK meetings and lynchings and could supply information known only to white observers. Under his direction the NAACP became more effective year by year.

317. Caste and Class in a Southern Town, by John Dollard. New York: Harper and Brothers, 1949. 34 (1949): 227-29.

A revised edition of a work which first appeared in 1937. The author is not so sure of his data as he was at first as, he says, in the South much is hidden behind great sets of defensive habits. His observations and conclusions are similar to those of Gunnar Myrdal in An American Dilemma. Though social change occurs slowly, the United States must get rid of caste which is an embarrassment before the rest of the world and a contradiction in our claim toward democratic leadership.

318. Segregation in Washington, by the National Committee on Segregation in the Nation's Capitol [sic]. Chicago: The Committee, 1949. 34 (1949): 229-31.

Prepared by a most scholarly staff of 89 distinguished citizens of both races, this report has aroused universal comment. Discrimination against blacks in restaurants and theatres, the continuance of ghettoes and slums, segregated schools, and employment only in menial service, are practices prevalent in the capital of the nation. Representatives of color from foreign countries are often subjected to humiliating treatment when mistaken for American blacks. Members of the committee which prepared this report have been subjected to abuse by those wishing to perpetuate such practices.

319. A Business Primer for Negroes, by William K. Bell. New York: William K. Bell Publications, 1949. 34 (1949): 231-32.

Though the author has no great record of success in business and the book is poorly organized and incomplete, it may serve some purpose in pointing out the shortcomings of many black businessmen which they must overcome to succeed. The book is made up of quotations and opinions of persons chiefly unknown. The author is mistaken in saying that it is easy for independent stores to compete with chain stores. Black businessmen as a majority have never been inclined toward cooperative buying. Though good advice is included here and there Mr. Bell does not explain how the black businessman may obtain essential capital and credit.

320. <u>Lincoln and the Baltimore Plot, 1861</u>, ed. by Norma B. Cuthbert. San Marino, Ca.: The Huntington Library, 1949. 34 (1949): 361-63.

Some historians have been inclined to make light of the allegation of a plot to assasinate Lincoln as he passed through Baltimore on his way to his inauguration. Relying on the Pinkerton papers, the editor establishes the seriousness of the conspiracy and the wisdom of Lincoln to agree, though reluctantly, to travel secretly through Baltimore a day ahead of schedule. The book brings out that in Washington, located in a pro-slavery area, Lincoln's life was always in danger. Though not connected with the 1861 attempt, the plot of 1865 finally succeeded.

321. <u>The Negro in the United States</u>, by E. Franklin Frazier. New York: The Macmillan Co., 1949. 34 (1949): 363-65.

In this volume Dr. Frazier emphasizes the black community and its interaction with other elements of American society. The author lays the background in a brief historical account. It must be borne in mind, however that the sociologist is not supposed to discover or present anything new but opinions and theories. Dr. Frazier leans heavily upon the works of others, in certain parts upon the works written or produced by the reviewer to the extent of citing or quoting them from page to page. The book shows some progress in Dr. Frazier's thinking though it is badly organized. Still he has collated useful information from many sources.

322. <u>The Negro's Adventure in General Business</u>, by Vishnu V. Oak. Yellow Springs, Oh.: The Antioch Press, 1949. 34 (1949): 365-67.

Magnates in the business world are not impressed by black enterprises, though recently a magazine reported that there are several black millionaires. This author has been concerned with lower levels of endeavor where he has found some struggling businesses worth considering. The book, however, seems like a survey of not great depth by a teacher inexperienced in business. The author is not pessimistic like black economists trained in Northern Universities who have learned that the Negro capitalist is a failure and an impossibility and are trying to mis-educate blacks accordingly.

323. <u>Progress in Negro Status and Race Relations, 1911-1946, The Thirty-five Year Report of the Phelps-Stokes Fund</u>, by Anson Phelps Stokes, Thomas Jesse Jones, J.D. Rheinallt Jones, and L.A. Roy. New York, N.Y., 1948. 34 (1949): 367-69.

This report implies that the Phelps-Stokes Fund has
been the impetus in the progress of blacks in the 20th
century. Nothing can be further from the truth. In
the first place they are only a small foundation.
What they could give or influence was carefully
distributed as a means toward their own end of black
control. Thomas Jesse Jones, the director, closed all
channels of philanthropy for blacks except through the
Phelps-Stokes Fund. Keeping an eye on meetings and
conferences he opposed or blocked measures which would
disturb his control. But he acted behind closed doors
and institutions were doomed before they knew what was
happening. The Fund never helped the NAACP. They are
dishonest to take credit for progress made in spite of
them not because of them.

324. A History of the Gold Coast, by W.E.F. Ward. London:
Allen and Unwin, 1948.
325. The Gold Coast, A Survey of the Gold Coast and
British Togoland, 1919-1946, by F.M. Bourret. Stanford,
Ca.: Stanford Univ. Press, 1949. 34 (1949): 372-74.

Recent research and anthropology have thrown light on
the Gold Coast which justifies these new works. The
first mentions errors in administration in the past
and the better understanding held today. The British
point of view justifies subjugation of the tribes and
refers to efforts of the natives to maintain their
territories as outrages. The second book stresses the
importance of the Gold Coast as revealed by WWI and
WWII. Statistics show an increase in schools and
social services. But the author passes lightly over
the restlessness of the natives clamouring for
autonomy.

326. Selective Service in North Carolina, by Spencer B.
King, Jr. Chapel Hill, N.C.: The Univ. of North Carolina
Press, 1949. 34 (1949): 472-74.

This volume is North Carolina's official record of the
Selective Training and Service Act from September 1940
to March 1947. Black draftees were kept apart from
the white which makes it possible to compare
statistics for each. More whites than blacks were
exempted because the whites were employed in war
industries. More blacks were rejected because of
mentality, illiteracy, physical defects and disease.
Woodson's review goes carefully into details of each
of these points. The author does not adequately
explain the causes of the disparity in the
deficiencies of blacks and whites. He leaves the
impression that these defects are racial rather than
environmental.

327. Codrington Chronicle: An Experiment in Anglican
Altruism on a Barbados Plantation, 1710-1834, ed. by Frank

J. Klingberg. Berkeley and Los Angeles, Ca.: Univ. of California Press, 1949.   34 (1949): 475-77.

> Col.   Christopher   Codrington   gave   his   Barbados plantation and 300 slaves to maintain the missionary enterprise of Christianizing and educating the blacks whose work would produce the income needed for the undertaking,   a   change   from   exploitation   to cooperation. Planters in the area objected to such spoiling of the slaves. While Codrington College fell short of the standards of the colleges of the day, its importance cannot be overestimated. It heralded a new day for blacks on British plantations.

328. <u>Africanisms in the Gullah Dialect</u>, by Lorenzo D. Turner. Chicago: The Univ. of Chicago Press, 1949. 34 (1949): 477-79.

> The Gullah dialect has been misunderstood as the speech of a backward people who could not easily learn the English language.   Not so!   The people recently from Africa and isolated on islands off the coast of South Carolina where they seldom saw outsiders, retained much of their native tongue in a conflict of cultures. Dr. Turner, a distinguished scholar, lived among them for several years. He traces West African words from a number of tribes, as many as 4000 traceable directly to African dialects. His scholarly work blazes a new trail in black studies.

329. <u>Medicine Throughout Antiquity</u>, by Benjamin Lee Gordon. Philadelphia: F.A. Davis Co., 1949. 34 (1949): 479-81.

> This work presents the progress made in medicine in Europe, Asia, and Egypt (the only part of Africa treated),   using   monuments,   temples,   statues,   and inscriptions for evidence in pre-history. The author believes that Greek medical structure was based on Egyptian. Africa, Australia, and the "Islands of the Seas" are treated only superficially. Woodson adds that black slaves continued African practices long after their coming to America and even today some blacks in the coastal Sea Islands and neglected parts of the South still practice magic.

330. <u>The History of Schools for Negroes in the District of Columbia, 1807-1947</u>, by Lillian G. Dabney. Washington, D.C.: The Catholic Univ. of America Press, 1949.   35 (1950): 89-91.

> On the border between pro-slavery and anti-slavery states, there were in the District of Columbia from the beginning those who favored co-education of the races and those who opposed and acted out their feelings. The opposed drove out the teachers, and

those in favor took in the students. The author treats of the beginnings of public schools for blacks and the opening of secondary schools and others. Woodson raises some questions which have not been answered, and he states, "the thorough work done by the Catholics among Negroes in the District of Columbia should have been given more emphasis in contradistinction to that of similar undertakings which were not so thoroughly carried out."

331. Afrique Occidentale Francaise, by J. Richard-Molard. Paris: Editions Berger-Levrault, 1949. 35 (1950): 94-95.

A brief but informative treatment of French West Africa which includes discussion of the surrounding area, its geology, physiography, flora and fauna. Through the eyes of Mohammedan conquerors and Arabic traders the author shows ancient kingdoms like Ghana, Manding and Songhai. He deals with the question of race (white/black) and also the native tribes briefly in regard to stature, language, religion, social and political institutions, etc. In the third section the author deals with "the French peace, economic status and concentration of population in urban centers" and closes with a summary of present day West Africa. The author does not go into the revolutionary tendencies of the natives who insist they can now manage their own affairs.

332. Lincoln Collector: The Story of the Oliver R. Barrett Lincoln Collection, by Carl Sandburg. New York: Harcourt, Brace and Co., 1950. 35 (1950): 213-15.

This book must be classified as one of the rare and valuable books on Lincoln. It contains documents collected by the most widely known Lincolniana collector, with interpretations and a biography of the collector. The illustrations are so excellent and well chosen that they could tell most of the story without the text. The work clarifies the meaning of the sectional conflict and many unsolved problems which have been in dispute.

333. The Negro in Northern Brazil: A Study in Acculturation, by Octavio da Costa Eduardo. New York: J.J. Austin [sic], 1949. 35 (1950): 215-17.

One of a series of monographs of the American Ethnological Society. The author concentrates on the State of Maranhao which borders on the Atlantic Ocean. His purpose was to discover whether urban or rural blacks had taken over more of European culture, concluding that it is difficult to say. African patterns among rural blacks include cooperative work, economic independence of women and successive common-law unions. In urban areas blacks have better preserved African religious practices. African beliefs persisted most strongly among Dahomeans and Yorubans.

334. <u>Mission to Haiti: Report of the United Nations Mission of Technical Assistance to the Republic of Haiti.</u> Lake Success, N.Y.: United Nations, 1949. 35 (1950): 217-19.

At the request of the Haitian government the U.N. sent a team of experts to make a survey of conditions in Haiti to determine what technical assistance she needed to improve her situation. The ten members found agricultural resources inadequate to the expanding population and a need for irrigation, drainage, flood-control, reforestation, economic, trade, and health reforms. The question is how these reforms will be financed as Haiti cannot possibly carry them out with her own present resources.

335. <u>African Dependencies: A Challenge to Western Democracy,</u> by Nwankwo Chukwuemeka. New York: The William-Frederick Press, 1850 [sic]. 35 (1950): 219-21.

The author, a Nigerian, teaching at Howard University, devotes most of this book to Nigeria, the dependency he knows best. Efforts at development there have been frustrated by economic imperialism. He exposes handicaps for those who live there and points out the inefficiency of the administration which is political rather than economic and social, and is conducted with a deficit costly to Great Britain and to the dependency. The U.N. should give dependencies representation. While the proposals made are wholly unacceptable to the exploiters, its appearance and the book's marks an epoch in African affairs.

REFERENCES TO WOODSON IN <u>THE JOURNAL OF NEGRO HISTORY</u>

336. Arnold, Edward F. "Some Personal Reminiscences of Paul Laurence Dunbar." 17 (1932): 400-408.

Arnold refers to his personal correspondence with Dunbar. Wanting to preserve these letters for posterity, he learned of the collection which Woodson had deposited in the Library of Congress and placed the letters in the Woodson collection. Arnold devotes a paragraph of about 175 words to Woodson and his work.

337. Bethune, Mary McLeod. "The Torch is Ours." 36 (1951); 9-11.

The speech of Mrs. Bethune at the first Annual Meeting of ASNLH after the death of Woodson showed warm appreciation of what the Founder accomplished. She affirmed that the results of his efforts vindicate the soundness of his thinking and demonstrate the necessity for the growth of ASNLH, the master key to the background of the world of color.

338. Cade, John B. "Out of the Mouths of Ex-Slaves." 20 (1935): 294-337.

This early experiment in oral history brings first-hand witness to the institution of slavery from living ex-slaves and ex-slave owners. The author compiled his article from 82 interviews. Page 306 has the story of the sale of Carter G. Woodson's grandmother, and pp. 319-320 the story of his grandfather's fight with an overseer and of his uncle's rebellion, punishment and sale.

339. "The Director's Survey of Research in Europe." 17 (1932): 504-506.

For three months in 1932 Woodson interviewed European scholars to determine how much interest they showed in Africa or Africans. In London he found the International Institute of African Languages and Culture white-dominated. He spoke in Louvain to a Catholic missionary society, held conferences in France and Germany and consulted with delegates to the League of Nations.

340. "Dr. Carter G. Woodson Studies the Negroes in Florida." 13 (1928): 222-23.

During February and March 1928 Woodson made a survey of social and economic conditions in Florida as they related to blacks. From Jacksonville he proceeded to Pensacola, then back to Tampa and Miami and the towns in between. The article enumerates those who assisted him and the places at which he spoke.

341. "A Duplication of Effort in Producing Two Encyclopedias of the Negro." 17 (1932): 116-18.

Woodson was not invited to the conference planning to publish an Encyclopedia of the Negro called by Anson Phelps Stokes for Nov. 7, 1931. Invited to the second meeting, Jan. 9, 1932, Woodson refused the invitation, explaining that the Associated Publishers had been compiling an Encyclopedia Africana and had begun the editorial work.

342. "Fiftieth Anniversary of the Journal of Negro History." 51 (1966): 75-97.

Tributes to the Journal of Negro History and to Woodson by William M. Brewer, Arthur M. Schlesinger, Sr., Charles H. Wesley, Merle Curti, John Hope Franklin, Leslie H. Fishel, Jr., Benjamin Quarles, James M. McPherson, Lorenzo J. Greene, Harvey Wish, Lorenzo D. Turner, Louis Ruchames, Dwight L. Dumond, Richard Bardolph, Frenise A. Logan, Kenneth M. Stampp, George Ruble Woolfolk, Eva B. Dykes, Barton J. Bernstein.

343. "The First Biennial Meeting of the Association for the Study of Negro Life and History at Washington." 2 (Oct. 1917): 442-48.

Held Aug. 29, 1917, the meeting was attended by distinguished white persons as well as prominent scholarly blacks. Woodson set forth the purpose of ASNLH in the expression so often repeated since: that the Negro may not, like the Indian, leave no written account of his thoughts, feelings, aspirations, and achievements. The Constitution, which is included, was ratified at this meeting.

344. Fontaine, W.T. "An Interpretation of Contemporary Thought from the Standpoint of the Sociology of Knowledge." 25 (1940): 6-13.

Fontaine delineates the movement of the black intelligentia away from traditional thought patterns, naming Woodson as one who has pointed out the sins of omission and commission in Dunning, Burgess, Rhodes, and others. The historic consciousness of the black scholar, he believes, is due to Woodson's reconstructed history.

345. Garrett, Romeo B. "African Survivals in American Culture." 51 (1966): 239-45.

Quotes a letter from Carter G. Woodson (Nov. 18, 1947) in which he states that he can see Africa in almost every black he meets--not referring to color; the "Caucasianization" of the Negro is far from complete.

346. Hesseltine, W.B. "A Quarter-Century of The Association for the Study of Negro Life and History." 25 (1940): 440-49.

Woodson by his contribution to scientific history through a reconsideration of the role of blacks in America, by challenging the Dunning picture of Reconstruction and forcing revisions of former concepts, made it impossible to accept the argument that blacks have been destined for an inferior role.

347. "John Morton Riddle." 27 (1942): 243-46.

John Morton Riddle, Carter Woodson's uncle and his first teacher, died on the 18th of March 1942. This obituary account contains extensive information about Woodson's family background and insights into the politics of Buckingham County, Va.

348. Johnson, Georgia Douglass. Review of Echoes from the Hills, by Bessie Woodson Yancey. 25 (1940): 107-108.

In praising this book of verses Georgia Johnson reveals sidelights on the family life of Woodson. Six years older than Bessie, he was working on the mines when his family moved back to Huntington in 1892. His father's work at the C&O Railroad and his principalship of the Douglass High School when Bessie graduated are mentioned.

349. Lindsay, Arnett G. "Manuscript Materials Bearing on the Negro in America." 27 (1942): 94-101.

When in 1937 the Committee on Historical Source Materials of the American Historical Association recommended a survey of institutions maintaining manuscript resources, specific work concerning black manuscripts was included on Woodson's recommendation and Lindsay was engaged to conduct it. The reference to Woodson here is brief but significant, and the project is closely related to the objectives of ASNLH.

350. Logan, Rayford W. "Carter G. Woodson: Mirror and Molder of His Time, 1875-1950." 58 (1973): 1-17.

Logan's article, a lecture delivered Oct. 21, 1972, discusses the extent to which Woodson reflected and changed the events of his time and makes a reaffirmation of and a rededication to his aims. Besides recounting Woodson's life the article demonstrates the continuity of ASNLH with the American Negro Academy and other efforts which preceded ASNLH.

351. L[ogan], R[ayford] W. "Personal: Carter Godwin Woodson." 35 (1950): 344-48.

An extensive account by Dr. Logan, who was then editing JNH, detailing the publication of Woodson's books, the progress made by ASNLH, and the conflict with Thomas Jesse Jones and Anson Phelps Stokes. The measurement of Woodson's achievement is seen in the current realization of the need for the revision of text books.

352. Logan, Rayford W. "Report of the Director." 35 (1950): 359-67.

Logan's report speaks of the death of Woodson and the impossibility of anyone else's performing the multitudinous tasks which he performed. The report gives the terms of Woodson's will, summarizes his plans, and explains that his purpose for Negro History Week was that it be a patriotic manifestation. Propaganda organizations and volcanic movements should be discouraged.

353. "Notes." 7 (1922): 120.

Mentions Dr. Woodson's current study of slavery from the point of view of the slave himself. He has sent out a searching questionnaire from which he has obtained some results, and is consulting records and documents also.

354. "Notes." 16 (1931): 250.

An obituary notice. Edward Channing, McLean Professor of History at Harvard, trained in history most of the black historians doing creative work. He early manifested interest in the work of ASNLH not only because he taught Woodson but because he believed that it had made a contribution to historical scholarship.

355. Paschal, Andrew G. "The Paradox of Negro Progress." 16 (1931): 251-265.

This long article develops many principles of education and ideas which Dr. Woodson advocated, and the author quotes him in three places to support his thesis of mis-education. Since education should fit individuals to their environment a youth should be trained to lay the foundation for the future in his present environment.

356. Wesley, Charles H. "Carter G. Woodson--As a Scholar." 36 (1951): 12-24.

Certain characteristics of a scholar were typical of Woodson: he was a discoverer of truth, a contributor to truth, an organizer of truth, a disseminator of truth, and a fighter for truth. Wesley develops each of these points at length, and mentions Woodson's marked intellectual ability in literary production.

357. Welsey, Charles H. "The Concept of Negro Inferiority in American Thought." 25 (1940): 540-60.

This long article comments on works published in the U.S. from the colonial era through the 20th century which label Negroes as inferior beings. Wesley credits Woodson and ASNLH with answering scientifically the absurd and irrational arguments which the advocates of race superiority have advanced.

358. Wesley, Charles H. "Creating and Maintaining an Historical Tradition." 49 (1964): 13-33.

Wesley reviews the progression in thought from the sense of inferiority engendered by jimcrow to the present, but sees no notable changes having occurred nationally until the pioneer endeavors of Woodson and his associates. At the core of the present Negro revolution are the teachings of the ASNLH based upon sound historical tradition.

359. Winston, Michael R. "Carter Godwin Woodson: Prophet of a Black Tradition." 60 (1975): 459-63.

"Father of Black History" does not summarize Woodson's career nor his accomplishments as an historian and editor. His importance now is greater than before because of the values underlying his work. They project a black tradition whose richness will be more fully actualized as a foundation of new progress in the future.

360. Woodson, Carter G. "Personal: John Franklin Jameson." 23 (1938): 131-33.

Jameson's obituary makes some references to Woodson.
Dr. Jameson once thought of adding him to his staff at
the Bureau of Historical Research of the Carnegie
Institution. However, his courage was not equal to so
unconventional a move in the face of prejudice. With
Dr. Jameson's cooperation Woodson secured in 1921 a
$25,000 grant.

3.
Negro History Bulletin

ARTICLES BY WOODSON IN THE NEGRO HISTORY BULLETIN

361. "The Negro in the West Indies." 4 (Jan. 1941): 76-77, 87-90.

   This article reads like an encyclopedia entry covering the discovery and exploration of the islands, the introduction of black slaves, claims by rival nations and raids by buccaneers and pirates. The account is brought up to the present with names of notable men from the islands.

362. "The Latin-American Background." 4 (Feb. 1941): 100, 111-14.

   A very long account of Spain's claims to America through the explorations of Columbus, her search for treasure, colonization and conflicts, the slave uprisings which led to the organization of maroons and eventual freedom, and the racial amalgamation of the region.

363. "The Longing for Foreign Lands." 4 (May 1941): 172, 183-84.

   Free blacks opposed the efforts of the American Colonization Society to remove blacks to Liberia or other countries, even though slave states expelled them for fear of their influence and free states objected to them because of employment problems. Some blacks did leave the U.S. but in general the ACS was a failure.

364. "The Anniversary Celebrated." 4 (June 1941): 198-99, 206-207, 215.

   A speech delivered on the 50th Anniversary of West Virginia State College, formerly West Virginia

Collegiate   Institute.   Woodson   points   out   the
historical development of its three   periods   and   gives
credit   to   its   pioneering   educators,   with   special
plaudits for President John W. Davis.

365. "The Negro in   New   England."   5   (Oct.   1941):   4-10,
22-23.

In   New   England blacks were never a large percentage of
the population.   Woodson   details   the   introduction   of
anti-black   legislation,   and   the   movement   for
abolition.   When   life   became   onerous,   some   blacks
escaped   to   the   Indians.   Others,   like   Paul Cuffee,
were   successful   and   prosperous.   Boston   produced
several black artists and professional people.

366. "The Negro in New York."   5 (Nov. 1941): 28-34.

Recounting   the   beginning   of   slavery (1650), attempts
at insurrection and reprisals, escapes   to   Canada,   and
abolition   (1827),   the   article   then   discusses   the
colonization   of   blacks   to   Liberia   and   its   loss   of
favor.   Progress   was   early   made   in   education
(Alexander   Hamilton   was   one   who   established   a
school).   Blacks have had many   successes   in   New   York
in spite of opposition.

367.   "The   Negro   in   the   Border   States."   5 (Jan. 1942):
76-82, 89.

This long, rambling article   stresses   mostly   Virginia,
the   District   of   Columbia   and Maryland.   In this area
slavery   existed   from   very   early   times   but   in   a
somewhat   milder   form   than   elsewhere.   Woodson   says
that   more   distinguished   blacks   came   from this area,
especially   Maryland,   from   any   other   part   of   the
country.

368. "Isaac Lane."   5 (Feb. 1942): 118.

Born   a   slave   in Tennessee, Lane had a kind master who
encouraged him to read.   After Emancipation,   the   white
planter   became   impoverished   and   Lane   bought   his
library.   In 1882 he founded Lane College of   which   his
son,   James   Franklin,   became president.   Isaac Lane was
made a bishop of the Colored Methodist Church in 1873.

369. "The Negro in the Land of   Cotton."   5   (Mar.   1942):
124-26, 140-42.

Beginning   with   the   relationship   between   blacks   and
Indians,   the   importance   of slavery to cotton, and the
cruelty   of   plantation life,   the   article   continues   to
post-Emancipation   and   elected   black   legislators,
post-reconstruction   conditions,   the   Freedman's Bureau,
Tuskegee Institute and   progress.   Lists   of   important
people are included.

370. "Democracy." 6 (Oct. 1942): 3-4, 14.

This article shows Woodson's cynicism and disillusionment with the U.S. government as a democracy, which, he says, is hampered by selfish politicians and trade unions while social distinctions and race prejudice flourish. People are not concerned about the label but about their opportunities to enjoy benefits without regard to race, creed, or color.

371. "The Slow Progress of Real Democracy." 6 (Dec. 1942): 51, 68, 70.

Over a long period of time democracy has made progress. Reformers demanded prison reform, adequate wages, temperance, woman suffrage, and public education. It required time to bring these things about.

372. "Stumbling Blocks to Democracy." 6 (Jan. 1943): 75, 89-91.

Politics, greed, race hate, class strife, sectionalism and religious prejudice are stumbling blocks. The attitude that the only hope for the weak is to become one of the strong further stimulates greed. Thus government is dictated by the rich. The gap between the rich and the poor develops class distinctions and prejudices.

373. "Essentials of Democracy." 6 (Feb. 1943): 100-101, 107, 119.

Listing the fundamentals of democracy, the article dwells on the ways in which they are denied blacks. But these rights would not be of much avail without land and a home. Government is run by the few who own the country, whose idea of democracy is the freedom to impose on one's fellow men.

374. "Democracy Always a Dream." 6 (Mar. 1943): 123-24, 142-43.

Woodson cynically explains how the rich become richer and the poor become poorer, through exploitation of the poor by the rich. Exploiters lavish money on a selected group of Negroes whom they then manipulate and publicize as leaders.

375. "Negroes Not United for Democracy." 6 (May 1943): 170, 177-78.

Payoffs by white segregationists lure ambitious blacks to barter the good of the race for personal advantage and to sign on the dotted line decisions already made. These blacks know what they are doing but are only concerned with their own selfish interests.

376. "In Spite of No Leadership the Negroes' Hope for Democracy Lingers." 6 (June 1943): 194, 213.

This long editorial expresses Woodson's cynical bitterness toward the so-called Christian Church and Christian educators who have instilled into blacks the conviction of their inferiority. Industrialism and economic forces have destroyed de facto slavery by bringing white and black workers together. Hope for democracy lies in the laboring classes.

377. "What's Behind 'The Negro History Bulletin.'" 7 (Oct. 1943): 16-20.

The NHB has a well-defined program supported in a literary and financial way by teachers, officials in the schools, and branch officers of the ASNLH. Pictures of 17 of these are shown and their distinct contributions mentioned. Woodson appreciated and acknowledged help received.

378. "Negro Women Eligible to be Daughters of the American Revolution." 7 (Nov. 1943): 36, 39.

The DAR is permeated by race prejudice. At least 3,000 black soldiers whose names are authenticated served in the Revolution. Among their descendents are such distinguished persons as Rose Leary Love, teacher and poet, and Charlotte Forten Grimké, a woman of great intellect. In spirit the DAR are descendents of the followers of George III.

379. "David Wilmot, a Man of Vision." 7 (Jan. 1944): 76.

David Wilmot's contribution to the anti-slavery struggle has been overlooked by historians chiefly because the best known American historians have glorified the pro-slavery leaders and branded the anti-slavery leaders as criminals. In the writings of such pseudo-historians, a worker for freedom such as Wilmot was soon forgotten.

380. "My Recollections of Veterans of the Civil War." 7 (Feb. 1944): 103-104, 115-18.

This autobiographical article gives details of Woodson's early life, his parents and relatives. It relates his father's experiences in the war and his discussions with a white Confederate veteran, Wysong, under whom he worked at the C&O Railroad shops. Oliver Jones, at the Nuttalsburg mines, George T. Prosser and P.B.S. Pinchback are included.

381. "Between Two Wars." 7 (Mar. 1944): 127-28, 142-43.

The Spanish-American War maintained oppression of

blacks in the U.S., though they fought valiently throughout. Victory spread the idea of color-caste into Cuba, Puerto Rico and the Philippines. Expensive clubs for whites only were organized with elegant club-houses from which blacks were excluded. Racial troubles increased.

382. "The Negro in the First World War." 7 (Apr. 1944): 147-48, 167.

In spite of opposition to arming blacks and efforts to restrict them to labor in the expeditionary force, officers trained at the special camp for blacks received the highest praise from French officials, and two blacks received decorations from the French for valor in action. But in the U.S. mob violence erupted against black soldiers.

383. "The Negro in the Present World Conflict." 7 (May 1944): 171-72, 190-91.

Jimcrow in the military supports the same policy as Nazi race superiority. Though the President's executive order to abolish discrimination in war industries was hailed as a new social order, industry disregarded it. The Fair Employment Practice Committee has accomplished some good. This article also discusses unions and the ballot.

384. "Gains and Losses in Retrospect." 7 (June 1944): 200, 202.

If the outcome of conflicts with Spain, England, and Mexico in America had been different, the situation for blacks need not necessarily have been improved. Even after the Civil War the North soon forgot the plight of the blacks and black soldiers returned from France to continued prejudice at home.

385. "Evident Developments of the War." 8 (Oct. 1944): 3-4, 21-22.

In the final stages of the war, governments and industrialists, after having wooed the cooperation of blacks with promises, now assert that, the emergency over, blacks must abandon their gains. British dominions especially can hope for little from the economic imperialists. But blacks will struggle to maintain the equality they have won.

386. "A Significant Outcome of the Present War." 8 (Nov. 1944): 27-28.

The U.S. military found that segregation destroyed efficiency and lowered morale. In spite of the vociferous exponents of jimcrow, numerous national officials see the inconsistencies of such policy. Blacks, far in advance of their 1919 status, have repudiated Uncle Tom leadership and have learned to use their own power.

387. "A New Definition of Social Equality." 8 (Dec. 1944): 51-52, 69.

One result of the war is a new definition of social equality. Released from bondage, blacks considered themselves as good as anyone else. But Southerners reacted with lynchings and massacres. The present war has shown that the southern code of white supremacy must be abandoned. Too high a price is being paid for prejudice.

388. "Universal Education: Another Development from the War." 8 (Jan. 1945): 75-76.

After the first World War some efforts to combat illiteracy were made in Germany, France and the U.S., but were not far-reaching or permanent. The present war has shown the importance of considering education a national matter. Some states object to education's becoming a political issue. Not much progress has been made internationally.

389. "Equality Before the Law." 8 (Feb. 1945): 99-100, 119.

In the lower South some whites are not so much concerned about winning the war as they are lest blacks become equal citizens. In spite of laws to guarantee blacks the enjoyment of all rights, inequities in the courts are numerous. The great decrease in the past year of lynchings is encouraging.

390. "Workers for Equality and Justice." 8 (Mar. 1945): 125-28, 141, 143.

This article enumerates outstanding black lawyers and the court cases in which they were involved. Young black lawyers today are as well qualified as their white counterparts and have obtained concessions from the Supreme Court in matters of housing, education and politics.

391. "Negro Historians of Our Times." 8 (Apr. 1945): 155-56, 158-59.

William C. Nell and George Washington Williams, early black historians, wrote with scientific objectivity. Some recent white historians who exalted slave-holders and southern aristocracy have been answered by black writers trained in scientific method. Modern black historians have expounded the history of the Negro.

392. "The History of the Department of Negro Affairs."   8
(May 1945): 172, 187-88.

Developing a clearer understanding of segregation,
blacks objected to a separate black unit in the D.C.
Fire Department and to government departments
appointing blacks in charge of "Negro Affairs" who
have no responsibility and are only buffers for
department heads. All affairs of government concern
blacks as much as any other citizen.

393. "A Foreign Faith in Protest." 8 (June 1945): 195-96,
215.

A bitter condemnation of hypocrisy in Christianity
according to which God ordained blacks to be menials
for superior whites. Blacks, rejected by
Christianity, find ready acceptance in Mohammedanism.
So-called Christians made blacks the objects of hate
and cruelty. The world needs a new revelation of God
to replace a system of hypocrisy.

394. "Making a Living in Africa." 9 (Nov. 1945): 33-36.

There are many classes of people in Africa, engaged in
many occupations. Agriculture, hunting, and fishing
are important, and cotton-growing, spinning and
weaving. Beautiful artistic productions are made of
ivory, stone, leather and metals, especially bronze.
Africans are learning European ways and rising in
business and the professions.

395. "Response." 9 (Dec. 1945): 64, 68-70.

Ohio, a most progressive state, has produced black
writers, inventors, and orators. Although Black Laws
prevailed in the southern part, the northern part
advanced the Underground Railroad. History shows that
the world was civilized from Africa where stringed
music, wall paintings, ivory carvings, and other
evidences attest to its ancient culture.

396. "An Advance in Diplomacy." 9 (Feb. 1946): 101-104.

The appointment of William H. Hastie, a lawyer, as
Governor of the Virgin Islands and R. O'Hara Lanier,
an educator, as Minister to Liberia recognizes the
black for his ability. In Liberia, founded by
American blacks, the post has been filled by white men
for the last quarter century and blacks filled only
subordinate roles.

397. "Haiti as Stable as France." 9 (Mar. 1946): 123-24,
143.

The Haitian record of self-government compares

favorably with that of its mother-country, France. Haiti has maintained its independence as a sovereign nation. This article gives a chronological overview of the history of each nation.

398. "The Record of the Clements." 9 (June 1946): 197-200.

Bishop George C. Clement produced a distinguished family, including his son Dr. Rufus E. Clement, president of Atlanta University. His widow, Mrs. Emma Clarissa Clement, was named the American Mother of 1946.

399. "Robert Thomas Kerlin Still Active at Eighty-One." 10 (Nov. 1946): 35, 47.

Mr. Kerlin's book, <u>Negro Poets and Their Poems</u> went into its fourth edition when he was eighty-one. This courageous white man lost at least three positions in colleges because of what his superiors considered over-interest in blacks. He fought all his life for liberty and freedom for all men.

400. "Lincoln as a Southern Man." 10 (Feb. 1947): 105-106.

Southern historians who contend that Lincoln, born in the South and married to a Southern woman, wished to restrict Negroes to the exercise of nominal freedom, are totally wrong. Neither Southerner nor Northerner, with the courage to follow what he believed right, Lincoln was the first to propose suffrage for literate freedmen who owned property.

401. "Honor to Booker T. Washington." 10 (March 1947): 123-29, 143.

Booker T. Washington became a world figure as a result of the speech containing the famous words "Cast down your buckets where you are" and "In all things that are purely social we can be as separate as the fingers..." The article includes this speech. Woodson's commentary describes the misunderstanding that followed its delivery. W.E.B. DuBois led the opposition of the "talented tenth" and Woodson gives a list of prominent Negroes pro and con Washington. But the Government minted a half million half dollars to be sold for $1.00 each, the extra 50¢ to go to purchase for a memorial the plantation where Washington was born. Woodson illustrated Washington's international renown by an autobiographical anecdote of an occurrence in Germany in 1907. To demonstrate that Washington's ideas about education were the same as those of Frederick Douglass, Woodson concludes with a speech made by Douglass.

402. "Choosing the Road Through Bloodshed." 10 (May 1947): 177-78.

Woodson examines the stand conservatives are taking
against Communism in America. He thinks that the
forceful elimination of Communists from U.S. service
is unconstitutional, and may lead to a one-party
system or to bloodshed. FDR, he says, made progress
in exterminating inequity, but the Conservatives have
reversed that policy.

403. "The Gibbs Family." 11 (Oct. 1947): 3-12, 22.

The family originated among the earliest citizens of
Philadelphia. Mifflin Wister Gibbs, in his
autobiography, Shadow and Light, gives some details.
A lawyer and judge, he became U.S. Consul in
Madagascar. His brother Jonathan became Secretary of
State of Florida. Many members achieved distinction,
among them Hunts, Marshalls, Laws, and Millers.

404. "Robert Smalls and His Descendants." 11 (Nov. 1947):
27-33, 46.

The hero, Robert Smalls, generated a distinguished
family. His daughter, Elizabeth Lydia, served as his
secretary when he was in Congress. She married Samuel
J. Bampfield who served in the South Carolina
legislature. They had eleven children. General
Smalls' descendants include Bampfields, Stinsons,
Boyds, Robinsons, Greenlees, Meyers, Davidsons,
Givens, and Boulwares.

405. "The Wormley Family." 11 (Jan. 1948): 75-84.

This family goes back as free persons of color to the
earliest days of the U.S. Pere Leigh Wormley moved to
Washington, D.C. in 1818 and operated a livery
stable. His son James became the well-known
proprietor of the Wormley Hotel, patronized by
statesmen and diplomats. Descendants include many
distinguished and useful citizens.

406. "The Waring Family." 11 (Feb. 1948): 99-107.

Captain William Waring, a Scotchman, settled in
Virginia about 1750. An officer in the Revolutionary
War, he produced a family of seven children by his
slave. Education or other field of service such as
medicine seemed an inheritance. Descendants include
Warings, Bakers, Williamsons, Steeles, Howards,
Frenches, and Bookers.

407. "The Cuney Family." 11 (Mar. 1948): 123-25, 143.

Of Indian, Swiss, and black descent, the Cuneys trace
their ancestry back to 1800. Several lawyers were
among the descendants and also an aggressive
politician who was influential in establishing a State

School for Deaf, Dumb and Blind Negroes. Maud Cuney-Hare was author of <u>Negro Musicians and Their Music</u>.

408. "The Bustill Family." 11 (Apr. 1948): 147-48, 167.

Cyrus Bustill (b. 1732), a baker who supplied troops of the American Revolution, a Quaker, whose daughter Grace established a Quaker millinery shop, had descendants active in abolition, the Underground Railroad, and civil rights. Grace Bustill Douglass's son became a portrait painter, and her daughter, also an activist, taught school for sixty years.

409. "More about John McKee." 11 (May 1948): 171-73.

McKee, a wealthy black Philadelphian, died in 1902 having lived modestly, never giving evidence of his riches. A landlord with 300 houses he always had a waiting list. He left only small bequests from his $1,000,000 estate to family members, and the rest to the Catholic Archbishop , who felt he should not accept it.

410. "Alice Victoria Weston and Her Family." 11 (June 1948): 195-98.

Alice V. Weston, of a family of distinguished achievements, became one of the prominent women of Kentucky. Her uncle was a judge in Philadelphia. She taught at Lincoln High School, Paducah, for 24 years. Active in the Kentucky State Association of Colored Women and Kentucky Negro Education Association, she was also devoted to ASNLH.

411. "Abyssinia." 12 (Nov. Dec. 1948, Jan. 1949): 35-38, 40-45, 67-71, 89-90, 92.

This long article in three parts reads like an encylopedia entry, covering in the first installment physical features, natural resources and trade (and including seemingly meaningless cross-references: e.g.: "Black Jews," q.v.) After King Theodore's efforts to modernize the country the article switches back to ancient times. The second installment is historical, from 1490 to 1916. The third, the shortest, tells of the accession of Haile Selassie, Mussolini's invasion, and the defeat of Italy.

412. "The Negro in Pennsylvania." 12 (Apr. 1949): 150-52, 167.

This article reads like an encyclopedia entry, describing physical features, products and industries. Quakers and Scotch-Irish Presbyterians are contrasted, the trouble between French and Indians

related, and the conflict between the later Irish
immigrants and blacks for jobs. Anti-slavery
societies arose. Names of many distinguished
Pennsylvanians are listed.

413. "The Negro in Early Virginia." 12 (May 1949):
173-80, 191.

The physical features of Virginia, the importation of
blacks, the government, and privately endowed black
colleges are described. (There is a useless q.v.)
The history of the state includes the code of laws
affecting blacks, Nat Turner's rebellion and John
Brown's raid, and secret societies, especially the
True Reformers.

414. "The Negro in Maryland." 12 (June 1949): 207-14.

To the Calverts is attributed the introduction of
slavery into Maryland. The Underground Railroad
allowed the escape of Frederick Douglass, Harriet
Tubman, J.W.C. Pennington, and Henry Highland Garnet.
Free blacks became educated and prosperous. A
separate long section on Baltimore includes the names
of prominent black Baltimoreans.

415. "Egypt." 13 (Nov. Dec. 1949, Jan. 1950): 39-45,
62-70, 95.

This long article considers the geography, climate,
people, government, archaelogical exploration, and art
of Egypt, before taking up in detail the history of
the country.

416. "Thaddeus Stevens." 13 (Dec. 1949): 51-52.

The article brings out Stevens's interest in blacks,
his work for the public schools of Pennsylvania, his
war on Andrew Johnson's Southern principles, and his
selection of his final resting place.

417. "French West Africa." 13 (Feb. Mar. 1950): 108-116,
129-32, 134-39.

The first section, very long, with bibliography
chiefly in French, details the geography of the
region, the conquests and slave trade which led to
French possession, and the forced labor which made the
region productive. Woodson gives separate accounts of
the history of Senegal and Dahomey with the names of
kings and princes and their achievements. In the
second section he gives detailed accounts of Ivory
Coast, French Sudan, French Guinea, Mauritania, Niger
and Haute-Volta.

REFERENCES TO WOODSON IN THE NEGRO HISTORY BULLETIN

418. "About the Founder." 25 (Feb. 1962): 120.

The article to accompany a cover photograph of Woodson presents his accomplishments and lists his books but omits mention of his years in the Philippines. It contains common errors: he attended the Sorbonne before the University of Chicago, and he received his B.A. from the University of Chicago in 1908 (not 1907).

419. "About the Founder--Carter Godwin Woodson." 23 (Feb. 1960): 120, 119.

A comprehensive summary of Woodson's life, which includes a listing of his books, is followed by his instructions for the celebration of Negro History Week.

420. Alexander, Raymond Pace. "Study of Negro Blasts Racial Myths. Judge Alexander comments on Textbooks in Letter to The Philadelphia Inquirer." 28 (1964): 3-6.

Replying to an article by Gerald Grant, "7 Texts Criticized for Negro Omissions," Judge Alexander praised the Inquirer for intelligent understanding and rated Woodson as one of America's greatest historians and the leading authority on the history of American blacks who frequently visited Harvard as guest lecturer and summer visiting professor.

421. Bethune, Mary McLeod. "True Leadership is Timeless." 13 (May 1950): 173.

An emotion-filled tribute from one who loved Carter Woodson and after close association with him for thirteen years declared him a prince among men. A testimony of faith in him because he moved back barriers and broadened visions.

422. "Biographical Sketch." 13 (May 1950): 171-73.

Reprint from Current Biography, February 1944.

423. Brooks, Albert N.D. "Dr. Woodson the Inspiration."
20 (1956): 72, 66.

At the dedication of the Carter G. Woodson High
School, Washington, D.C., November 19, 1956, Brooks
designated Woodson as a great teacher who supplied
motivation and inspiration to black youth through his
researches in history. His life and work inspire
youth to rise to their highest potential.

424. Cobb, W. Montague. "Carter Godwin Woodson,"   36
(1973): 151-55. Rpr. Journal of the National Medical
Association, 62, No. 5 (Sept. 1960).

Woodson's vision, perceived at a time hostile to his
efforts, inspired his work through arduous years of
single-minded purpose and Spartan living. Dr. Cobb, a
generation younger, had many enriching contacts with
Woodson and states that his gain has been as much from
Woodson's wisdom as from his writings.

425. "Completing the Cycle." 25 (May 1962): 170, 181-82.

Narrates Woodson's struggle to obtain funds for the
Association and refers to his own frugal life style
which enabled him to contribute so much personally.
Tells of the attempts after his death to carry on the
Association and describes the current program in
progress.

426. "The Death of the Founder." 13 (May 1950): 170, 176.

An account of Woodson's funeral services and
survivors, followed by an appreciation from the
Phillis Wheatley YWCA which identifies him with the
poem beginning "Let me live in a house by the side of
the road." Woodson's friendship with the residents of
the Y was warm and informal. They call him a lofty
soul, a profound scholar, a perfect gentleman,
generous, thoughtful, and benevolent, with a store of
anecdotes of wit and humor.

427. "Ebony Honors Association's Founder." 21 (Mar.
1958): 144. Rpr. Ebony, Feb. 1958.

Woodson is included in the Ebony Hall of Fame for the
great legacy of his writings. It is impossible for
anyone to do serious study of black history without
studying his material, the editorial states, and
stresses his affection for children and his wish for
them to appreciate their potentialities.

428. "Editorial: The American Negro Academy (1897-1916); The Black Academy of Arts and Letters (1969-1970)." 33 (Nov. 1970): 156-57.

The American Negro Academy, composed of distinguished and scholarly blacks, pursued its ideals until 1916. The Black Academy of Arts and Letters, founded to emulate the ANA, held its First Annual Awards Banquet Sept. 10, 1970. Sidney Poitier presented Carter G. Woodson for the Black Academy's Hall of Fame. Also presented were Henry O. Tanner and W.E.B. DuBois.

429. "Editorial: Black Studies and History Week." 35 (Feb. 1972): 28-29.

Through the efforts of Carter G. Woodson, especially through Negro History Week, the role of black history has expanded to become Black Studies, with departments in many schools. But hurried responses to the demand have led to propagandistic application, distortions and use of inferior materials. Negro History Week should promote only historical truth.

430. "Editorial: Teaching Black History." 32 (Mar. 1969): 4-6.

In 1903 John Spencer Bassett wrote "Stirring Up the Fires of Racial Antipathy" in which he urged a new approach to the study of the black American. Ten years after this controversial article, Woodson planned his association to bring about this end. The editorial relates its founding and his rationale for the study of blacks in our history.

431. "Editorial: What's in a Name--Negro, African, Black, Afro-American, Colored, Black-American or Negro-American." 34 (Feb. 1971): 28-29.

Article X of the Constitution requires a 2/3 vote at the Annual Meeting for amendment, after notification of members at a previous annual meeting. In 1970, a name change was approved against an active objecting minority. A statement by W.E.B. DuBois explaining the word Negro and a history of the word are included.

432. Franklin, John Hope. "The Place of Carter G. Woodson in American Historiography." 13 (May 1950): 174-76.

Following Reconstruction some racist historians were accomplices in the program to degrade blacks to a permanent position of inferiority and drive them out of politics. Woodson was well qualified to challenge their fantastic claims and to become the historian of black people. His contributions have initiated a significant and far-reaching movement.

433. "George Edmund Haynes." 23 (Oct. 1959): 2, 21.

In his Memoir, Haynes describes his friendship with
Woodson, who visited him at Fisk in 1914 and discussed
his dream of an association to promote the study of
Negro life and history and a publication to preserve
historical records. He also mentions later occasions
when Woodson discussed his plans with him.

434. Greene, Lorenzo J. "Dr. Woodson Prepares for Negro
History Week, 1930." 28 (Summer 1965): 174-75, 195-97.

Entries from Greene's diary for January 1930 narrate
the struggle of the Negro History Week Committee to
arrange for a "monster" celebration bringing together
all available black congressmen. Discussions of
banquet date, costs, and arrangements, program format
and printing, and other practical matters bring out
interesting facets of Woodson's character.

435. Hay, Samuel A. "Carter G. Woodson's Mis-Education of
the Negro: A Re-visit." 38 (Aug.-Sept. 1975.): 436-39.

Negro History Week and Woodson's writings influenced
the author in his youth. He states the thesis of The
Mis-Education of the Negro: that American education
teaches the black man to hate himself. Evidence in
1975 supports Woodson's conclusions of 1933. Hay sums
up Woodson's views as the highest and most practical
of ideals.

436. Hughes, Langston. "When I Worked for Dr. Woodson."
13 (May 1950): 188.

Hughes describes his daily routine and his special
task of alphabetizing the thousands of names in Free
Negro Heads of Families. Woodson's office staff
respected and admired him but wondered how he kept up
the pace of his work.

437. Jackson, Marian [sic.] "The History and Significance
of Negro History Week." 27 (Dec. 1963): 72, 70-71.

Coal miner, educator, historian and author, Woodson
set in action a great mass movement in 1926 by
launching Negro History Week. Marion Jackson Pryde,
his cousin, describes his career before briefly
developing a history of the Baptist Church. She
concludes: never did anyone with so little bring
self-respect to so many.

438. "Julia Davis." 25 (Apr. 1962): 168, 166.

The St. Louis Public Library received $2,500 from Miss
Davis for black studies. Her letter to Albert Brooks,
editor of NHB, tells how her association with Woodson

influenced her.   An enclosed news item refers to a
meeting she arranged for Woodson to meet Mr. Judge
Boggs of the St. Louis Public Schools.

439. Klingberg, Frank J. "A Salute to Carter G. Woodson."
19 (Dec. 1955): 50-51.

Klingberg, in lauding Woodson's accomplishments and
importance, describes the philosophy and rationale
behind his unceasing research.   He points out
Woodson's revisionist chapters on the contributions of
blacks to the Reconstruction of southern state
constitutions, the share of gifted black delegates to
these conventions, and their achievements in public
education.

440. Lindsay, Arnett G. "Dr. Woodson as a Teacher."   13
(May 1950): 183, 191.

Arnett Lindsay describes how he alone survived of
Woodson's five graduate students in the newly
established graduate school at Howard University of
which Woodson was dean.   Strict and serious, Woodson
lectured for hours without notes, bringing out the
romance of American history and adding spice to its
teaching.

441. Martin, Tony. "Carter G. Woodson and Marcus Garvey."
40 (1977): 774-77.

Contemporary with Garvey, Woodson pursued a different
path from his but understood Garvey's aims.   He wrote
a weekly column for Negro World in 1931 and 1932, and
Garvey reviewed Woodson's books in those pages.   They
were alike in ideas of self-reliance, race pride, and
independence of white support and influence.

442.   "Louis   Mehlinger--Secretary-Treasurer   of   the
Association for the Study of Negro Life and History."   15
(Oct. 1951): 18-19.

Captain Mehlinger, then a file clerk at the office of
the Treasurer of the United States, met Woodson when
he first came to Washington and took a room adjoining
Louis Mehlinger's in a rooming house on 11th Street.
They became close friends and collaborators.

443. Mays, Benjamin E. "I Knew Carter Woodson."   44
(Jan./Feb./Mar. 1981): 21.

The President Emeritus of Morehouse College calls
Woodson a legend in his own time and a challenge for
us today.   He narrates an incident when Woodson spoke
in Tampa, Florida, and another in Paris.   He says
Woodson did for the black what Gandhi did for the
Hindu.

444. Milton, Nerissa L. "A Thought for Christmas." 27 (Dec. 1963): 68.

Each year at Christmas Woodson himself composed the greeting on his Christmas card. Frank J. Klingberg said that Woodson's cards were the only ones he preserved from year to year. The article quotes one of the cards.

445. "Negro History and the Advancement of Negro Masses." 22 (Dec. 1958): 72, 71.

Education is the magic lamp of our time, especially in the interdependent trilogy of philosophy, science and history. Carter G. Woodson saw the importance of fitting the pieces of history together scientifically and that science and history can demonstrate the basic equality of blacks.

446. Poitier, Sidney. "Sidney Poitier on Carter G. Woodson." 33 (Nov. 1970): 158.

The remarks made by Poitier on presenting Woodson for the Hall of Fame at the First Annual Awards Banquet of the Black Academy of Arts and Letters, New York Hilton Hotel, Sept. 20, 1970, besides listing his achievements recall his selflessness, foresight, persistence and steadfast commitment to black people.

447. Quarles, Benjamin. "The Associated Publishers." 28 (Jan. 1965): 81.

A detailed account of Woodson's organizing the Associated Publishers, its purpose and achievements.

448. Reddick, L.D. "As I Remember Woodson." 17 (Nov. 1953): 36-38.

As a boy in Jacksonville, Florida, Reddick first saw Woodson and heard him speak. He describes the impression the great man made on him. Later, as a teacher, he came to know Woodson personally, visited and talked with him. From frequent encounters Reddick points out the qualities and characteristics which distinguished Woodson.

449. Reddick, Lawrence D. "Twenty-Five Negro History Weeks." 13 (May 1950): 178-79, 188.

Woodson was surprised and elated at the immediate success of Negro History Week. It quickly became popular and not only in black institutions. He made it clear that he did not wish the occasion to be exploited for the financial benefits of other organizations nor used for unrelated propaganda purposes.

450. Roy, Jessie H. "Some Personal Recollections of Dr. Woodson." 28 (Summer 1965): 185-86, 92.

This tribute gives insight into the impression Woodson made on high school students, and later on two collaborators in his work. Teachers in the D.C. Public Schools, Jessie Roy and Geneva Turner completed a book for Woodson shortly before his death. He admitted to them that he was getting old and had not been feeling well.

451. Scally, Sister Anthony. "The Carter Woodson Letters in the Library of Congress." 38 (June/July 1975): 419-21.

The Carter G. Woodson Collection of Negro Papers and Related Documents in the Library of Congress is in 16 boxes. Two of these contain chiefly letters to Woodson. The article surveys a sampling of these, showing how they furnish interesting sidelights on black history.

452. Scally, Sister Anthony. "Over the Mountains." 38 (Dec. 1975): 474-77.

The saga of Woodson's young parents, going on foot across the mountains, from New Canton, Virginia, to Huntington, West Virginia, to work on the new railroad. A reconstruction of their laborious journey as it must have been.

453. Scally, Sister Anthony. "The Philippine Challenge." 44 (Jan./Feb./Mar. 1981): 16-18.

An account of Woodson's four years of teaching in the Philippine Islands, told chiefly from correspondence in the National Archives, Washington, D.C.

454. Scally, Sister Anthony. "Woodson and the Genesis of ASNLH." 40 (Jan./Feb. 1977): 653-55.

The events that led to the establishment of ASNLH and the rough first two years, 1915-1917, as shown in the correspondence between Dr. Jesse Moorland, the first treasurer of ASNLH, and Dr. Woodson. Reference is made to Du Bois' suggestion that the NAACP take over the JNH and Woodson's rejection of the offer.

455. Stamps, James E. "The Beginning of the Association for the Study of Negro Life and History." 29 (Nov. 1965): 31-32.

In recounting the first meeting and founding of ASNLH James E. Stamps, one of the five present, reveals aspects of Woodson's character as well as the political and social background of the times.

456. Taylor, Alrutheus A. "Dr. Carter G. Woodson, Inspirer and Benefactor of Young Scholars." 13 (May 1950): 186, 189.

By the inspiration of his work and example and in more tangible ways Woodson was a benefactor of young scholars. He trained some to be investigators for the Association, secured funds for others for advanced studies, assisted candidates to develop doctoral dissertations, and made available the facilities of the Association.

457. Thompson, Charles H. "An Unusual Personal Experience with Carter G. Woodson." 13 (May 1950): 185.

Thompson first met Woodson in Chicago, June 1926, when Woodson received the Spingarn Medal. Thompson was much impressed by Woodson's speech of acceptance. In 1935 he and Mrs. Thompson met Woodson in Paris. They made a dinner engagement at which Woodson was host and discovered a gourmet Woodson they had not known existed.

458. Thorpe, Earl E. "Africa in the Thought of Negro Americans." 23 (Oct. 1959): 5-10, 22.

Discusses the controversy which has arisen over the extent to which African traits remain in the thought and actions of Afro-Americans. The article, giving the attitudes toward Africa of blacks as divergent as Phillis Wheatley and Marcus Garvey, includes the opinions of Woodson, and quotes frequently from his works. The author also discusses the attitudes of other black writers, musicians and artists toward Africa.

459. Turner, Geneva C. and Jessie H. Roy. "Bridging a Gap." (documentary for television.) 20 (Mar. 1957): 133-37.

A dramatization of a visit of two teachers to the ASNLH offices in preparation for Negro History Week. During the visit they meet the staff of the Association and hear the story of Carter G. Woodson and of the founding and purpose of the ASNLH.

460. Wesley, Charles H. "The Association and the Public." 17 (Jan. 1954): 75-78.

In delineating the Association's responsibility not only to the scholarly segment of the population but to the general public as well, Dr. Wesley asks all members to see that the boys and girls and others of the communities in which they are located realize the truth of African ancestry. He pays tribute to Dr. Woodson as founder, states the purposes of branches as

Woodson gave them, and relates some of his achievements.

461. Wesley, Charles H. "Our Fiftieth Year." 28 (Summer 1965): 172-73, 195.

The year 1965 marks two milestones for blacks: the 100th year since the adoption of the 13th Amendment and the 50th year of ASNLH. A summary of Woodson's career and the history of the founding of ASNLH, the article stresses Woodson's individualism which led him to go much of his way alone.

462. Wesley, Charles H. "Resurgence in Africa's Historical Tradition and the American Reaction." 24 (Jan. 1961): 81-89.

An address at the 45th Annual Meeting of ASNLH in Austin, Texas, Oct. 18, 1960, credits Woodson with leading the resurgence of historical truth about Africa through the work of ASNLH. Wesley mentions especially The African Background Outlined. Though devoting only about 300 words to Woodson, he shows the importance of Woodson in the general movement.

463. Wesley, Charles H. "Retrospect and Prospect." 13 (May 1950): 192, 189-91.

Woodson made the cause of Negro History his primary relationship with amazing self-denial. Generous in praise, fearless in decisions, and discriminating in judgment, a pioneer and organizer, he laid the foundation for brotherhood in a nation of mixed races and creeds.

464. Woodson, Carter G. "My Recollections of Veterans of the Civil War." 7 (Feb. 1944): 103-104, 115-18.

See no. 380.

465. Young, Alfred. "Historical Origin and Significance of the Afro-American History Month Observance." 45 (No. 4, 1982): 100-101.

An exposition of the central idea of Negro History Week as established by Woodson, and his systematic effort by this and other means to instill a sense of pride in Afro-Americans, and to inform the public of their past history. Celebrations were not to play up grievances but to demonstrate achievements.

4.
In Books

SELECTIONS FROM WOODSON'S WORKS IN BOOKS

466. "The Anniversary Celebrated." In <u>Major Addresses,</u> <u>Delivered on the Occasion of the Semi-Centennial</u> <u>Celebration of West Virginia State College</u>. 7-8, 21-24. Semi-Centennial Series Publication No. 1, Series 3, no. 3. Institute, W.Va.: West Virginia State College Press, Aug.-Nov. 1941.

   See no. 364.

467. Aptheker, Herbert, ed. <u>A Documentary History of the</u> <u>Negro People in the United States</u>. Vols. 1 and 2. New York: Citadel Press, 1951, 1973.

   Both volumes draw on the works of Woodson. Vol. 1
   uses five selections from Woodson's works. Vol. 2
   reprints two articles by Woodson and two selections
   from his edited works.

468. Davis, John W., ed. <u>Problems in the Collegiate</u> <u>Education of Negroes</u>. 14-15, 20, 29. West Virginia State College Bulletin, Dept. of Education, no. 8. Institute, W.Va.: West Virginia State College, 1937.

   This pamphlet of 56 pages presents varying points of
   view brought together to bear on the subject of
   collegiate education in an informal uninterpreted
   compilation. Dr. Davis wrote to a selected group of
   persons asking that each indicate three major problems
   in the area. Woodson was one of the contributors,
   indicating problems in "Coordinating Effort,"
   "Curriculum," and "Articulation."

469. <u>Dictionary of American Biography</u>, ed. Dumas Malone. New York: Charles Scribner's Sons, 1928-1937.

   "Richard Allen," vol. 1; "Richard Henry Boyd," vol. 2;
   "John Mifflin Brown," "Morris Brown," "William Wells

Brown," "Blanche K. Bruce," "Richard Henry Cain," vol. 3; "George Wylie Clinton," vol. 4; "Henry Highland Garnet," "Richard Theodore Greener," vol. 7. In an article (New York Age, June 18, 1932) Woodson explained that he resigned from the staff of DAB when the editor refused to spell Negro with a capital, omitted Benjamin Banneker as unworthy of mention, and branded John Brown as a lunatic.

470. DuBois, W.E.B. The Correspondence of W.E.B. DuBois, ed. Herbert Aptheker. Vol. 1, Selections 1877-1934, 140, 449. Amherst, Mass.: Univ. of Massachusetts Press, 1973.

Two letters by Woodson to DuBois, the first as a student at the University of Chicago, asking the help of DuBois for his thesis on the Negro Church; the second, refusing to participate in plans for an encyclopedia of the Negro.

471. "Excerpts from a Speech by Carter G. Woodson. Tuskegee Institute, ca. 1930." In Thelma D. Perry, History of the American Teachers Association, 195-98. Washington, D.C.: National Education Association, 1975.

This speech may be much earlier than the estimated 1930. References to meekness and patience would indicate this, as well as poetical allusions to singing a new song to the universe so that man will forget his conflict. The total absence of Woodson's usual cynicism indicates that he had not yet become disillusioned.

472. "Extracts from Fifty Years of Negro Citizenship." In Anthology of American Negro Literature, ed. V.F. Calverton, 412-35. New York: The Modern Library, 1929.

This selection discusses the Supreme Court in relation to the Dred Scott Decision and the Fugitive Slave Law, and after the Civil War the 13th and 14th Amendments and the Civil Rights Bill. The dissenting opinion of Justice Harland is presented.

473. "Foreward." Calendar of the Writings of Frederick Douglass in the Frederick Douglass Memorial Home, Anacostia, D.C. Washington, D.C.: Historical Records Survey, W.P.A., 1940. Under the supervision of Arnett G. Lindsay.

A short essay in which Woodson stresses the importance of preserving documents, especially those of Douglass who ranks first in importance. All phases of his activity are represented in these papers: abolition, temperance, women's suffrage, prison reform, and labor. Woodson portrays the vision and wisdom of Douglass in his agreement and disagreement with his famous contemporaries, and his disillusionment in post-bellum developments.

474. "Free Negro Owners of Slaves, 1830." In <u>From Freedom to Freedom, African Roots in American Soil</u>, ed. Mildred Bain and Ervin Lewis, 262-64. New York: Random House, 1977.

In 1830 free blacks had reached their highest peak as a separate class, and were about 1/7 of those in the country. Many slaves held by free blacks were their wives or husbands obtained by purchase, or children of the slave wife, to be emancipated later. Affluent free blacks enjoyed the same social standing and privileges as their white counterparts. By 1840 the trend towards degrading free blacks was apparent. See no. 7.

475. Hill, Adelaide Cromwell and Martin Kilson, comp. and eds. <u>Apropos of Africa; Sentiments of Negro American Leaders on Africa from the 1800's to the 1950's</u>. London: Frank Cass and Co., 1969.

"Carter Godwin Woodson," a biographical account, is reprinted from Kelly Miller's <u>An Estimate of Carter G. Woodson</u> and is followed by "African Superiority," reprinted from an undated clipping. See no. 536.

476. "History and Propaganda," an address delivered in Baltimore, February 10, 1926. In <u>Readings from Negro Authors for Schools and Colleges</u> with a Bibliography of Negro Literature, by Otelia Cromwell, Lorenzo Dow Turner, Eva B. Dykes, 303-307. New York: Harcourt, Brace and Co., 1931.

In 1926 when this speech was made the ASNLH was a young organization and Woodson had to sell the idea of its importance. Here he made two of his best-known statements justifying his organization: "If a race has no history, if it has no worthwhile tradition, it becomes a negligible factor in the thought of the world, and it stands in danger of being exterminated." And: "In the broad view of history the achievements of the Negro properly set forth will crown him as a factor in early human progress and a contributor to modern culture." Race prejudice is the outcome of indoctrination that blacks have never contributed anything to the progress of mankind. Blacks learned this lesson and recognized their inferiority. This is propaganda which justifies the domination and exploitation of the weak by the strong.

477. "History Made to Order." In <u>The Negro Caravan</u>, ed. Sterling A. Brown, Arthur P. Davis, and Ulysses Lee, 839-46. New York: The Dryden Press, 1941. Repr. Arno Press and the New York Times, 1969.

In "History Made to Order," Woodson refutes Eaton's distortion of facts regarding slaves who returned to the South from persecution in the North, the church as

it developed in the South, and southern
abolitionists. This shortened version omits several
references contained in the JNH article. See no. 32.

478. "History Made to Order." In The Negro Since
Emancipation, ed. Harvey Wish. Englewood Cliffs, N.J.:
Prentice-Hall, 1964.

In the introduction to this selection, Dr. Wish offers
an opinion of Woodson's significance in the general
picture of black historiography. The essay,
originally presented in JNH, is valuable for a
statement of Woodson's ideas on slavery and
abolition. See no. 32.

479. "Introduction." In Negro History in Thirteen Plays,
by Willis Richardson and May Miller. Washington, D.C.:
Associated Publishers, 1935.

An introductory essay expressing Woodson's opinion of
the state of current theater, which he considered
stagnant and rife with racial propaganda. Blacks
could, like Molière in the seventeenth century, bring
about a change by portraying the real drama of
America, their own lives. The playwrights in this
volume have taken this step toward emancipation of the
mind of the black from the slavery of inferiority
complex.

480. "Introduction." In Pioneers of Long Ago, by Jessie
Hailstalk Roy and Geneva Calcier Turner. Washington, D.C.:
Associated Publishers, 1951.

In this introduction Woodson speaks of the necessity
of teaching blacks out of their own background and the
lack of such literature. He praises the authors of
this book for presenting unexaggerated truth in such a
dramatized way as to hold the interest of the children
for whom the work is intended.

481. "Letters Written During the Crisis." In From Freedom
to Freedom: African Roots in American Soil, ed. Mildred
Bain and Ervin Lewis, 285-88. New York: Random House, 1977.

Selections from The Mind of the Negro as Reflected in
Letters Written During the Crisis, 1800-1860 includes
a letter to Rev. J.W. Logan from his former mistress
(Apr. 27, 1860) which blames subsequent family
misfortunes on him for taking the mare and running
away. She tells "Jarm" that she has sold his brother
and sister, and threatens to sell him unless he sends
her money. His reply (Mar. 28, 1860) is a masterpiece
of outrage and indignation. The selection includes
three other letters.

482. "Lily-White Lincoln." by Francis J. Grimké. In A Documentary History of the Negro People in the United States, vol. 2, no. 28. Secaucus, N.J.: Citadel Press, 1973.

Selection from The Works of Francis J. Grimké, vol. 1, ed. by Carter G. Woodson. The reference is to Lincoln University.

483. "The Mis-education of the Negro." In A Documentary History of the Negro People in the United States, vol. 2, no. 143. Secaucus, N.J.: Citadel Press, 1973.

From The Crisis 38 (Aug. 1931): 266-67. See no. 593.

484. "A Negro Denounces Prejudice Within the Abolitionist Movement, 1837." In A Documentary History of the Negro People in the United States, vol. 1. New York: Citadel Press, 1951. Repr. from C.G. Woodson, ed. Negro Orators and Their Orations. Washington, D.C.: Associated Publishers, 1925.

An oration by Theodore S. Wright at the Convention of the New York State Anti-Slavery Society.

485. "Negro Education." In Encyclopedia Americana, vol. 20. New York: Encyclopedia Americana Corp., 1919.

The article surveys the conflict between blacks, their sympathetic friends and the missionaries brought in to educate the blacks, and the more successful efforts of most planters to keep them ignorant. A description of progress after the civil war, with statistics and names of benefactors, follows.

486. "Negro Fighters for Freedom and Unity 1863-1865." In A Documentary History of the Negro People in the United States, vol. 1. New York: Citadel Press, 1951. repr. from C.G. Woodson, ed. The Mind of the Negro as Revealed in Letters Written During the Crisis, 1800-1860. Washington, D.C.: Associated Publishers, 1926.

A letter from Frederick Douglass' son, Lewis Douglass, a member of the 56th Massachusetts Infantry Regiment [Volunteers], to his fiancee.

487. "Negro Slavery." In European Civilization: Its Origins and Development, 7 vols., The Relations of Europe with Non-European People, v. 7: 553-93, ed. by Edwin Eyre. New York: Oxford Univ. Press, 1934-1939.

The article has four parts: Trading in Men, The Negro Enslaved, Slavery and World Movements, and Observations and Comparisons. The first section describes the need for cheap labor in the New World, the development of the slave trade, and the African tribes from which the victims came. The second section compares slavery in different regions, and the third tells the relation of slaves and freedmen to the social upheavals of the time.

488. "The Negroes of Cincinnati Prior to the Civil War." In Free Blacks in America, 1800-1860, ed. by John H. Bracey, Jr., August Meier, and Elliott Rudwick, 70-84. Belmont, Cal.: Wadsworth Publishing Co., 1971.

From JNH 1 (Jan. 1916): 1-22. See no. 23.

489. "The Negro's Response to Colonization, 1817-1818." In A Documentary History of the Negro People in the United States, vol. 1. New York: Citadel Press, 1951. Repr. from C.G. Woodson, ed. The Mind of the Negro as Revealed in Letters Written During the Crisis, 1800-1860. Washington, D.C.: Associated Publishers, 1926.

A letter by Abraham Camp, an Illinois free black, to Elias B. Caldwell, Secretary of the Colonization Society, indicative of the minor opinion of blacks, most of whom repudiated the idea of colonization.

490. "A Philadelphia Negro Condemns Discriminatory Proposals, 1813." In A Documentary History of the Negro People in the United States, vol. 1. New York: Citadel Press, 1951. Repr. from C.G. Woodson, ed. Negro Orators and Their Orations. Washington, D.C.: Associated Publishers, 1925.

A letter by James Forten.

491. "Some Things Negroes Need to Do." In A Documentary History of the Negro People in the United States, vol. 2, no. 84. Secaucus, N.J.: Citadel Press, 1973.

From Southern Workman 51 (Jan. 1922): 33-36. See no. 595.

492. "A Symposium on Garvey." In A Documentary History of the Negro People in the United States, by Herbert Aptheker, vol. 2. New York: Citadel Press, 1973. Repr. from Messenger 4 (Dec. 1922).

Chandler Owens sent a letter and questionnaire to 25 prominent blacks noting that Garvey had met with Ku Klux Klan leaders and that A. Philips Randolph had received a human hand in the mail accompanied by a letter from the Klan telling him to join Garvey's organization. Owens asked if the respondents thought Garvey's policy was correct for blacks and if they thought he should be deported. Woodson's brief reply is given.

493. "Too Ready to Sacrifice Our Rights," by Francis J. Grimké. In <u>A Documentary History of the Negro People in the United States</u>, vol. 2, no. 18. Secaucus, N.J.: Citadel Press, 1973.

Selection from <u>The Works of Francis J. Grimké</u>, vol. 3, <u>Stray Thoughts and Meditations</u>, ed. by Carter G. Woodson.

494. "Twenty-Five Years of Higher Education Among Negroes." In <u>Higher Education Among Negroes</u>, ed. by Theophilus Elisha McKinney. Charlotte, N.C.: Johnson C. Smith Univ., 1932.

Shortly after the Civil War public schools for black children developed largely through the efforts of blacks themselves. Philanthropy financed higher education in such colleges and universities as Howard, Hampton, Johnson C. Smith, Atlanta, Dillard and Fiske. Advocates of industrial training and those of classical education disputed their respective advantages without either side coming out ahead, as neither prepared blackss for the real life situation they had to face.

REFERENCES TO WOODSON IN BOOKS

In Reference Books:

495. <u>Chronological History of the Negro in America</u>, ed. Peter M. Bergman. New York: New American Library, 1969.

496. <u>Current Biography: Who's News and Why 1944</u>. New York: H.W. Wilson, 1954.

497. <u>Dictionary of American Biography. Supplement Four 1946-1950</u>, ed. John A. Garraty and Edward T. James. New York: Charles Scribner's Sons, 1974.

498. <u>Dictionary of American Negro Biography</u>, ed. Rayford W. Logan and Michael R. Winston. New York: W.W. Norton and Co., 1982.

   Dr. Logan mistakenly calls Carter G. Woodson "the oldest of nine children." My research shows him the seventh of nine, two children having died previously in Huntington before the family returned to New Canton where Carter G. Woodson was born.

499. <u>Encyclopedia of American Biography</u>, ed. John A. Garraty and Jerome L. Sternstein. New York: Harper, 1974.

500. <u>National Cyclopedia of American Biography</u>. New York: James T. White, 1953. Vol. 38.

501. <u>Negro Almanac</u>, ed. Harry A. Ploski and Ernest Kaiser. New York: Bellweather Co., 1971.

502. <u>Who's Who in America: A Biographical Dictionary of Notable Living Men and Women in the United States</u>. Chicago: Marquis, 1926-1950.

   Woodson was in <u>Who's Who in America</u>, 1926 through 1950.

503. <u>Who's Who in Colored America, a Biographical Dictionary</u> <u>of Notable Living Persons of Negro Descent in America</u>. New York: Who's Who in Colored America Corp., 1933, 1937, 1940, 1944.

504. <u>Who Was Who in America: A Companion Biographical</u> <u>Reference Work to Who's Who in America, Vol. 3</u>. Chicago: Marquis, 1960.

505. <u>International Library of Negro Life and History</u>, Robinson, Wilhelmina S. <u>Historical Negro Biographies</u>. New York: Publishers Co., 1967. [Under the auspices of the Association for the Study of Negro Life and History.]

> This account fails to mention Woodson's work in the Philippines, places his studies at the Sorbonne after his Ph.D. from Harvard, gives the date of his B.A. from the University of Chicago as 1907, and mistakenly gives his middle name as "Goodwin."

<u>In Other Books</u>:

506. Ambler, Charles H. <u>A History of Education in West</u> <u>Virginia, from Early Colonial Times to 1949</u>. Huntington, W.Va.: Standard Printing and Publishing Co., 1951.

> Ambler calls Woodson one of West Virginia State College's ablest teachers and organizers and says that under him as dean the college department was put upon a scholarly foundation. He quotes extensively from Woodson's "Anniversary Address." Woodson, Ambler says, pioneered the field of productive research.

507. "The Amenia Conference of 1916." In <u>A Documentary</u> <u>History of the Negro People in the United States</u>, vol. 2. Secaucus, N.J.: Citadel Press, 1973.

> Woodson was one of the fifty leaders invited to be guests of Dr. J.E. Spingarn, Aug. 24-16, 1916, at this historic meeting.

508. Aptheker, Herbert, ed. <u>A Documentary History of the</u> <u>Negro People in the United States</u>. 2 vols. New York: Citadel Press, 1951, 1973.

> In the Introduction to Vol. 1, Aptheker acknowledges Woodson as his constant inspiration whose writings, advice and friendship were among the most precious influences of his life. In the preface DuBois refers to the long hammering of Woodson to call attention to black history. In the preface to Vol. 2, Wesley states that only ASNLH, under the leadership of Woodson, achieved the objective of several previous black historical associations. Woodson's attendance at the Amenia Conference is noted in Vol. 2.

509. Bardolph, Richard. The Negro Vanguard. New York: Random House, Vintage Books, 1959.

Bardolph refers to Woodson as the race's foremost historian. He calls him the father of modern black historiography, who was venerated by scholars of both races, and considers JNH the major repository for black studies.

510. Broom, Leonard and N.D. Glenn. The Transformation of the Negro American. New York: Harper and Row, 1965.

Contains a discussion of cultural nationalism and shows how that concept applies to Woodson.

511. Brown, Sterling A., Arthur P. Davis and Ulysses Lee. The Negro Caravan. New York: The Dryden Press, 1941, repr. Arno Press and the New York Times, 1969.

A 300-word biography, listing many of Woodson's books, and characterizing him as combining the interest of a scholar with that of an organizer and journalist, precedes the essay "History Made to Order." In the preface of this book several of Woodson's books are mentioned, The Mind of the Negro as Reflected in Letters Written during the Crisis, 1800-1860, as being especially useful in preparation of the anthology.

512. Bullock, Ralph W. In Spite of Handicaps. New York: Association Press, 1928. Repr. Freeport, N.Y.: Books for Libraries, 1968.

A short biography in this collection begins with an encomium by Kelly Miller which cites Woodson's distinction between the history of the Negro and the Negro in history. It names Woodson's professors at the Sorbonne and at Harvard, but makes no mention of his years in the Philippines or his time at Howard. Distinguished men who endorsed ASNLH are named.

513. Butcher, Margaret Just. The Negro in American Culture, 2nd ed. Based on materials left by Alain Locke. New York: Alfred A. Knopf, 1972.

Woodson is credited with opening up new perspectives upon the African past, and with DuBois, insisting on the importance of restoring the African background. Butcher says he laid down the model for all studies for pre- and post-Civil War years. She briefly summarizes his life and mentions some of his books.

514. Cruse, Harold. The Crisis of the Negro Intellectual. New York: William Morrow and Co., 1967.

Woodson is mentioned in this study in three places: (1) the Communist Party attempts, through the

researches of Herbert Aptheker, to take over Negro
History Week, completely bypassing Dr. Woodson; (2)
the black bourgeoisie absorbs little from the few
thinkers it has produced, a group which includes
Woodson; (3) Aptheker's historiography is much like
Woodson's. He is only incidentally Marxist.

515. Cruse, Harold. <u>Rebellion or Revolution</u>. New York:
William Morrow and Co., 1968.

Cruse discusses the controversy between Booker T.
Washington and W.E.B. DuBois, and Woodson's position
toward each protagonist. He calls attention to
Woodson's stand in <u>The Mis-education of the Negro</u>
where he apparently favors the Washington school of
thought and does not mention DuBois, though elsewhere
he seems to downgrade DuBois' elitism.

516. Daedalus. <u>The Future of the Black College</u>. 100
(Summer 1971).

In scattered mention C. Eric Lincoln refers to
Woodson's influence in cultural change; Michael R.
Winston credits Woodson as a major force in
stimulating research among blacks and gives an
extensive biographical account; and Elias Black, Jr.
refers to the initiative generated by the tradition of
Carter G. Woodson.

517. Drimmer, Melvin, ed. <u>Black History: A Reappraisal</u>.
Garden City, N.Y.: Doubleday and Co., 1968.

A collection of essays published between 1945 and the
late 1960's to provide new insights into black
history. Woodson is credited in the introduction and
in several selections. Includes Shepperson's "Notes
on Negro-American Influences on the Emergence of
African Nationalism" annotated under periodicals. See
no. 625.

518. DuBois, W.E.B. <u>The Correspondence of W.E.B. DuBois</u>,
ed. Herbert Aptheker. Vol. 1, <u>Selections 1877-1934</u>; vol.
2, <u>Selections 1934-944</u>; vol. 3, <u>Selections 1944-1963</u>.
Amherst, Mass.: Univ. of Massachusetts Press, 1973.

In vol. 1 a letter to John Hope proposes Woodson as
the Spingarn Medalist for 1925. DuBois praises
Woodson's achievements as "a marvelous
accomplishment." Other letters in vol. 1 throw light
on Woodson's refusal to collaborate on a history of
blacks in the World War or on the encyclopedia of the
Negro. In vol. 2, DuBois recommends Woodson's books
to an inquirer, and in a letter to Dr. R.E. Park
discusses the proposed encyclopedia. In vol. 3,
DuBois makes proposals to Dr. Rayford Logan for the
ASNLH, and further discusses the encyclopedia with Dr.
Wesley.

519. Dyson, Walter. <u>Howard University the Capstone of Negro Education. A History: 1867-1940</u>. Washington, D.C.: The Graduate School Howard Univ., 1941.

A paragraph (p. 182) considers Dr. Woodson's work in the reorganization of the graduate school at Howard. On p. 183 notice is taken of Arnett G. Lindsay, Dr. Woodson's graduate student, M.A. 1920, and the subject of his thesis.

520. Feldman, Eugene Pieter Romayne, ed. <u>Figures in Black History</u>. Chicago: Du Sable Museum of African History, 1970.

A well-focused brief account which brings out Woodson's interest in destroying the inferiority complex of black youth and the importance of his well-documented materials.

521. Foster, William Z. <u>The Negro People in American History</u>. New York, International Publishers, 1954.

This book, written from a Marxist-Leninist viewpoint, under the heading "National Negro culture" identifies Negro History Week as an important factor in the research in and writing of black history, and credits Carter G. Woodson and the ASNLH with stimulating this trend. He also lists as leaders in the movement several Marxist historians.

522. Frazier, E. Franklin. <u>The Negro in the United States</u>. New York: Macmillan Co., 1949.

Frazier expresses disagreement with Woodson regarding evidences of African survivals in black American culture, but relies on him heavily in other subjects: education, the church, miscegenation, the ante-bellum free black, post-war freedmen, and business. Woodson is listed 14 times in Frazier's bibliography.

523. Gilbert, Peter, comp. and ed. <u>The Selected Writings of John Edward Bruce: Militant Black Journalist</u>. New York: Arno Press and the New York Times, 1971.

An entry from Bruce's diary in which he criticizes A. Philip Randolph for the socialist stand he took in the address he gave before the American Negro Academy, and dissents from Woodson's evaluation of Randolph as the leader of tomorrow.

524. Hamilton, Charles V. <u>The Black Preacher in America</u>. New York: William Morrow and Co., 1972.

The author refers to Woodson's "seminal study." <u>The History of the Negro Church</u>, and quotes a paragraph referring to all kinds of concerns demanded of the black preacher. Referring to ministry during slavery,

Woodson's defence of Peter Williams, Jr. is quoted, as well as his explanation of the break from the white Methodists to form the AME Zion Church.

525.   Harlan, John Clifford. History of West Virginia State College, 1891-1965. Dubuque, Ia.: William C. Brown Book Co., 1968.

There are three brief references to Woodson, indicating his place on the faculty, and later making an address during the Semi-Centennial Celebration.   He quotes from and lists in the bibliography Woodson's "Early Negro Education in West Virginia."

526. Hill, Adelaide Cromwell. "Africa Studies Programs in the United States." In Africa Seen by American Negroes. Presence Africaine, 1958.

Woodson [at the time] was the most widely read writer in the field of black history. His The Negro in Our History presented data previously unknown on the history of the American black and underscored his/her African origin.   The first four chapters of this volume are devoted to the role of Africa in history.

527.   Hughes, Langston. The Big Sea, an Autobiography. New York: Hill and Wang, 1940, 1963. (American Century Series.)

Dr. Woodson employed young Langston Hughes as his personal assistant in the offices of ASNLH.   Hughes found it much harder work than the laundry where he had previously worked.   One of his chores was to alphabetize the names for Woodson's work, Free Negro Heads of Families, and later to check the proofs.

528.   Isaacs, Harold R. The New World of the Negro American. New York: John Day Co., 1963.

In this book which purports to show the impact of world affairs on the race attitudes of black Americans, Woodson is mentioned ten times, most references being to the influence of his books on persons interviewed by the author. Devoted to the same purpose as Herskovits, to close the cultural gap between American blacks and their African background, both worked to re-establish a heritage in America and Africa for blacks to take pride in.

529. Lee, Ulysses. "The ASNLH, the Journal of Negro History and American Scholarly Interest in Africa." In Africa Seen by American Negroes. Presence Africaine, 1958.

After surveying the interest of American blacks in, and writings about, Africa prior to the establishment of ASNLH, and analyzing inclusions about Africa in the first issue of JNH, Lee gives a biographical account of Woodson and further analyses in <u>JNH</u>. While seldom naming Woodson, it is plain that the credit he gives to the Association pertains to Woodson as well.

530. Logan, Rayford W. "The American Negro's View of Africa." In <u>Africa Seen by American Negroes</u>. Presence Africaine, 1958.

Woodson, more than anyone else popularized interest in Africa among blacks in the United States. Through the annual meetings of ASNLH, the <u>JNH</u>, and especially through Negro History Week, he made known to the general public the history of ancient Ghana and other flourishing ancient kingdoms.

531. Logan, Rayford W. <u>Howard University, The First Hundred Years, 1867-1967</u>. New York: New York Univ. Press, issued under the auspices of Howard Univ., 1969.

Woodson's appointment and dismissal are mentioned, but no reason given for his demanded apology. There are three other brief mentions.

532. Maloney, Eugene A. <u>A History of Buckingham County</u>. Dillwyn, Va., Buckingham Co., Bicentennial Commission, 1976.

This brief history contains interesting material about the place where Woodson was born and where he lived until his late teens. The author devotes three pages to Woodson and his achievements.

533. Martin, Tony. <u>Race First; the Ideological and Organizational Struggles of Marcus Garvey and the Universal Negro Improvement Association</u>. Contributions in Afro-American and African Studies, no. 19. Westport, Conn.: Greenwood Press, 1976.

The four references to Woodson are short, but significant in defining his attitude toward Garvey and the UNIA, his place as a columnist for <u>Negro World</u>, and his avoidance of becoming involved in attacks on Garvey.

534. Meier, August. <u>Negro Thought in America 1880-1915. Racial Ideologies in the Age of Booker T. Washington</u>. Ann Arbor, Mich.: Ann Arbor Paperbacks, Univ. of Michigan Press, 1971.

Meier considered that the roots of the New Negro developed in the age of Booker T. Washington. He briefly summarizes Woodson's background, and mentions his scholarly achievements and the organization and purpose of the ASNLH which were, he says, characterized by ethnic dualism and the philosophy of the pre-war generation.

535. Meier, August and Elliot M. Rudwick. <u>From Plantation to Ghetto</u>. American Century Series. New York: Hill and Wang, 1966, rev. ed., 1970.

Contains a brief discussion of Woodson's fundamental beliefs regarding the African heritage; i.e., it was significant and worthy of study and it was enduring in America. The authors say that ASNLH places on scholarly foundations the investigation of both the African and the American past.

536. Miller, Kelly. <u>An Estimate of Carter G. Woodson and His Work in Connection with the Association for the Study of Negro Life and History, Inc.</u> Washington, D.C.: The Association for the Study of Negro Life and History, 1926.

In this early pamphlet Miller completely omits all mention of Woodson's work in the Philippines and of his organization of the Associated Publishers, but he lists Woodson's outstanding professors at the Sorbonne and at Harvard. The value of the account lies in Miller's analysis of Woodson's philosophy and the rationale of his sacrifices.

537. Moss, Alfred A., Jr. <u>The American Negro Academy, Voice of the Talented Tenth</u>. Baton Rouge: Louisiana State Univ. Press, 1981.

This study of the American Negro Academy mentions Woodson dozens of times. Woodson became a member of the ANA in 1913 or 1914. Good informal relations existed between the ANA and the ASNLH which he founded the following year. His break with ANA came in 1921 when the work of a three-member subcommittee on constitution revision, of which Woodson was a member, was rejected by ANA. The rejection seemed to indicate that ANA was not serious about resolving its conflict of goals, and as a result many members became inactive.

538. Myrdal, Gunnar. <u>An American Dilemma, the Negro Problem and Modern Democracy</u>; with the assistance of Richard Sterner and Arnold Rose. 2 vols. New York: Harper and Brothers, 1944.

Myrdal relies heavily upon Woodson when treating of migration and blacks in the professions. Discussing the Negro history movement, he gives great importance to the ASNLH and quotes Reddick to the effect that black historiography could be classed "before Woodson and after Woodson." He quotes at length from Woodson's <u>History of the Negro Church</u>.

539. "The Negro a Factor in the History of the World." Extension of remarks of Hon. Arthur W. Mitchell of Illinois in the House of Representatives. Wednesday, February 7, 1940. <u>Congressional Record, Appendix</u>, 627-29. Washington, D.C.

Includes a letter from Congressman Mitchell to Dr. Woodson and Woodson's reply. Often asked about black achievements, Mitchell wrote to Dr. Woodson for information. In his letter he tells Woodson he has been asked to speak in a dozen states on fifty occasions for Negro History Week. Woodson, in his long reply, touches on explorers, inventors, soldiers, artists, orators and educators, mentioning persons in all categories.

540. Perry, Thelma D. "Accent on Negro History." Chapter 10 in History of the American Teachers Association. Washington, D.C.: National Education Association, 1975.

Mrs. Perry discusses Dr. Carter G. Woodson, the Father of Negro History, his writings, and the work of the Associated Publishers, especially the books for children in whom Woodson took intense interest. She also includes excerpts from a speech by Woodson given at Tuskegee Institute "ca 1930." See no. 471.

541. Porter, Dorothy B. "A Bibliographical Checklist of American Negro Writers about Africa." In Africa Seen by American Negroes. Presence Africaine, 1958.

Woodson is mentioned among those whose writings have contributed notably to the knowledge of Africa's recent past. Dr. Porter lists three books and two articles of his.

542. Posey, Thomas E. The Negro Citizen of West Virginia. Institute, W.Va.: Press of West Virginia State College, 1934.

Much of Chapter VIII, "The Education of the Negro in West Virginia," depends largely on Carter Woodson's study of the early education of blacks in West Virginia. Woodson is credited with dividing the progress of education into three periods and for naming many outstanding pioneer teachers. Among these is his uncle, Robert D. Riddle. The bibliography lists four items by Woodson.

543. Record, Wilson. The Negro and the Communist Party. Studies in American Negro Life, August Meier, gen. ed. Univ. of North Carolina Press, 1951. Repr. Westport, Conn.: Greenwood Press, 1980.

The Communists attempted to woo blacks into the party by way of black history, especially through the pen of Herbert Aptheker who used reinterpretation by Carter G. Woodson and the ASNLH for propaganda purposes. The Communist challenge to steroetyped versions focused on relevent questions and opened avenues of discussion.

544. Rogers, Joel Augustus. "Carter G. Woodson." In
World's Great Men of Color, ed. with an intro., commentary
and new bibliographical notes by John Hendrik Clarke, vol.
2. New York: The Author, 1947. Repr. The Macmillan Co.,
1972.

This short account mentions Woodson's head injury in
the coal mines and also includes an interesting
quotation of a statement which Woodson made in 1932,
but without documentation. Rogers characterizes
Woodson as the great pioneer in the popularizing of
black history and the most voluminous writer and
editor on that subject.

545. Rollins, Charlemae Hill. "Carter Goodwin Woodson,
1875-1950, Scholar, Historian." In They Showed the Way,
Forty American Negro Leaders. New York: Thomas Y. Crowell
Co., 1964.

A short biographical account of Dr. Woodson which,
like many short accounts, is somewhat confused in its
time frame. For example, the date of his B.A. is
given as 1907 when the records show it as March 1908;
and his attendance at the Sorbonne is placed after his
receiving the M.A. from the University of Chicago.
However, this short account shows the spirit that
animated Woodson better than many other short accounts.

546. Scally, M.A., Walking Proud, The Story of Dr. Carter
Godwin Woodson. Washington, D.C.: The Associated
Publishers, 1983.

This biography by Sister Anthony Scally covers
Woodson's life from his birth in New Canton, Va., to
his sudden death in his room above the ASNLH offices.
It is a factual study based on original research, and
though written on the junior high school level, can be
read profitably and enjoyably by adults. It contains
a bibliography and an index.

547. Shuey, Audrey M. The Testing of Negro Intelligence.
New York: Social Science Press, 1966.

In a discussion of selective migration as affecting
differences in intelligence of northern and southern
blacks, the author cites writers who found that
Woodson's data contradicted his theory. This is an
interesting critique of A Century of Negro Migration.

548. Thorpe, Earl E. Black Historians. New York: Morrow,
1971.

Dr. Thorpe gives a biographical account of Woodson and
a study of each of his works. His time frame for
Woodson's childhood and youth is, like most condensed
biographies, somewhat garbled, but the review of each

book is very useful. He constantly pairs DuBois and
Woodson and in the study of many of the other
historians he reverts to Woodson's opinion; e.g. in
regard to B.T. Washington's The Story of the Negro,
Woodson considered the effort valuable. Or he states
that the historians worked with or were acquainted
with Woodson; e.g. Luther P. Jackson, John E. Bruce,
etc. To Woodson's organized movement he credits the
national attention given to black history.

549. Thorpe, Earl E. The Central Theme of Black History.
Durham, N.C.: Seeman Printery, 1969.

Thorpe early credits Woodson with launching the Negro
history movement. Except for two essays reprinted
from other works, "The Father of Black History" from
Negro Historians in the U.S. and "The Philosophy of
Black History" from The Mind of the Negro: An
Intellectual History of Afro-Americans, he mentions
Woodson only in passing, but makes frequent references.

550. Thorpe, Earl E. The Mind of the Negro: An
Intellectual History of Afro-Americans. Baton Rouge, La.:
Ortlieb Press, 1961.

Woodson's name occurs throughout this book. Dr.
Thorpe refers to his influence toward an understanding
of slavery, his knowledge of the Negro Church, and his
extensive researches in black history. He credits
Woodson with launching the black history movement
which, during the 20's, produced all forms of literary
expression.

551. Thorpe, Earl E. Negro Historians in the United
States. Baton Rouge, La.: Fraternal Press, 1951.

An earlier edition of Black Historians. See no. 548.

552. Toppin, Edgar A. A Biographical History of Blacks in
America Since 1528. New York: David McKay Co., 1971.

Dr. Toppin explains why Woodson was the premier
Afro-American historian and deserves to be called
Father of Black History. The account, however,
credits Carter Woodson with persuading his brother
Robert to go to Huntington, when, on the contrary, his
family and friends have testified that Robert, who was
older, went first and came back to get Carter. Dr.
Toppin shows a strong-willed, devoted historian
engaged in herculean labors for a cause he loved.

553. U.S. Library of Congress. Report of the Librarian.
Washington, D.C.: United States Government Printing
Office, 1929, 1930, 1933.

The 1929 report mentions 200 interesting documents

ranging from 1804-1927 deposited by Carter G. Woodson. In the 1930 report, a paragraph describes Woodson's "valued gift" to the Library of Congress, and the 1933 volume reports his addition to the "interesting collection."

554. Wesley, Charles H. The Quest for Equality, from Civil War to Civil Rights. (International Library of Negro Life and History.) Publishers Company, 1968, under the auspices of ASNLH.

Wesley mentions Woodson's founding of ASNLH and the publication of JNH as a factor in black progress. In a separate place he lists some of Woodson's books, and in another Woodson's concern for courses in black history.

555. Wish, Harvey. The American Historian, a Social-Intellectual History of the Writing of the American Past. Westport, Conn: Greenwood Press, 1983. Repr. Oxford Univ. Press, 1960.

Referring to Woodson's offense at U.B. Phillips' racialism and black stereotypes, Dr. Wish praises the accomplishments of Woodson and his contribution to raising the status of black historical studies to a high professional level.

556. Wolters, Raymond. The New Negro on Campus, Black College Rebellions of the 1920's. Princeton, N.J.: Princeton Univ. Press, 1975.

Treating of James Stanley Durkee's administration of Howard University and his conflicts with Woodson and other faculty and students, Wolters makes reference to the influence of Carter G. Woodson's educational ideas during his one year as Dean of the College and explains Woodson's resignation from Howard. The extensive account given here makes clearer Woodson's position at Howard.

557. Wright, C. Ruth. "Negro Authors Week: An Experiment." In A Documentary History of the Negro People in the United States, vol. 2. Secaucus, N.J.: The Citadel Press, 1973.

From The Crisis 38 (Apr. 1931): 124. See no. 633.

558. Writers' Program. Virginia. The Negro in Virginia. The American Negro His History and Literature, William Loren Katz, gen. ed. New York: Hastings House, 1940. Repr. Arno Press and the New York Times, 1969.

In Chapter 18, "War," a paragraph describes how James Woodson, Carter Woodson's father, slipped away from his slave master to join General Philip Sheridan's forces. Chapter 25, "Arts," includes Woodson in the account of Virginia writers, with a brief biography and a listing of his books.

559. Young, James O. *Black Writers of the Thirties*. Baton Rouge, La.: Louisiana State Univ. Press, 1973.

This survey of writers who flourished in the depression decade explores the tensions between the older race leaders and younger men influenced by other factors than race. While giving much space to Woodson, Young devotes most attention to his newspaper contributions, and while referring to him as "the noted historian," considers him a romantic black nationalist race man, with nineteenth-century middle-class values, who blatantly manifested black chauvinism and whose writings were essentially propagandistic.

Brief Mentions:

560. Aptheker, Herbert. *Essays in the History of the American Negro*. New York: International Publishers, 1945.

561. Aptheker, Herbert. "Introduction" to *Black Reconstruction*, by W.E.B. DuBois. Millwood, N.Y.: Kraus Thomson Organization, 1976.

562. Baraka, Imamu Amiri (LeRoi Jones) ed., *African Congress. A Documentary on the First Modern Pan-African Congress*. New York: William Morrow and Co., 1972. "Resource Papers. Education." by Acklyn Lunch. (Congress of African Peoples, Atlanta, 1970).

563. Bennett, Lerone, Jr. *Before the Mayflower: A History of the Negro in America, 1619-1964*. Rev. ed. Baltimore, Md.: Penguin Books, 1966. First pub. Johnson Publishing Co., 1962.

564. Bennett, Lerone, Jr. *Black Power U.S.A. The Human Side of Reconstruction 1867-1877*. Baltimore, Md.: Penguin Books, 1967.

565. Bullock, Henry Allen. "A Hidden Passage in the Slave Regime." In Curtis, James C. and Lewis L. Gould, eds. *The Black Experience in America, Selected Essays*. Austin, Tex.: Univ. of Texas Press, 1970.

566. [Cansler, Charles W.] Three Generations. *The Story of a Colored Family of Eastern Tennessee*. Privately printed, 1939.

567. Carlisle, Rodney P. *Prologue to Liberation: A History of Black People in America*. New York: Apple-Century-Crofts; Meredith Corp., 1972.

568. Chrisman, Robert and Nathan Hare, comp. <u>Contemporary Black Thought, the Best from "The Black Scholar."</u> Indianapolis/New York: The Bobbs-Merrill Co., 1973.

569. DuBois, W.E.B. <u>Black Reconstruction</u>. New Intro. by Herbert Aptheker. Millwood, N.Y.: Kraus-Thomson Organization, 1976. Repr. 1935 ed., Harcourt, Brace and Co., N.Y.

570. Franklin, John Hope. <u>From Slavery to Freedom, A History of Negro Americans</u>. 3rd ed. New York: Vintage Books, a division of Random House, 1969. Alfred A. Knopf, 1947.

571. Glenn, Norval D. and Charles M. Bonjean, eds. <u>Blacks in the United States</u>. San Francisco: Chandler Publishing Co., 1969.

572. Herskovits, Melville J. <u>The Myth of the Negro Past</u>. New York: Harper and Brothers, 1941.

573. Ikonne, Chidi. <u>From DuBois to Van Vechten: the Early New Negro Literature, 1903-1926</u>. Westport, Conn.: Greenwood Press, 1981. (Contributions in Afro-American and African Studies, No. 60.)

574. Johnson, Abby Arthur and Ronald Maberry Johnson. <u>Propaganda and Aesthetics; the Literary Politics of Afro-American Magazines in the Twentieth Century</u>. Amherst, Mass.: The Univ. of Massachusetts Press, 1979.

575. Johnson, Charles S. <u>The Negro College Graduate</u>. College Park, Md.: McGrath Publishing Co., 1969. Repr. Univ. of North Carolina Press, 1938.

576. Lincoln, C. Eric, ed. <u>The Black Experience in Religion</u>. Garden City, N.Y.: Anchor Press/Doubleday, 1974.

577. Logan, Rayford W. <u>The Betrayal of the Negro, from Rutherford B. Hayes to Woodrow Wilson</u>. New York: Collier Books, 1965. Orig. <u>The Negro in American Life and Thought: The Nadir</u>. Macmillan Co., 1954.

578. Quarles, Benjamin. <u>The Negro in the Making of America</u>. New York: Collier Books, a division of the Macmillan Co., 1964.

579. Redding, Saunders. <u>The Lonesome Road. The Story of the Negro's Part in America</u>. Garden City, N.Y.: Doubleday and Co., 1958.

580. Reimers, David M. <u>White Protestantism and the Negro</u>. New York: Oxford Univ. Press, 1965.

581. Robinson, Armstead L., ed. <u>Black Studies in the University: A Symposium</u>. New Haven, Conn.: Yale Univ. Press, 1969.

582. Silberman, Charles E. Crisis in Black and White. New York: Vintage Books, a division of Random House, 1964.

583. Torrence, Ridgely. The Story of John Hope. New York: Macmillan, 1948.

584. Van Deusen, John G. The Black Man in White America. Washington, D.C.: Associated Publishers, 1938.

585. Williams, Kenny J. They Also Spoke: An Essay on Negro Literature in America, 1787-1930. Nashville, Tenn.: Townsend Press, 1970.

586. Wilmore, Gayraud S. Black Religion and Black Radicalism. Garden City, N.Y.: Doubleday and Co., 1972. (C. Eric Lincoln Series on Black Religion.)

5.
In Periodicals

ARTICLES BY WOODSON IN PERIODICALS

587. American Negro Slavery. A survey of the supply, employment, and control of Negro labor as determined by the plantation regime, by Ulrich Bonnell Phillips, Ph.D., professor of American History, Univ. of Michigan. New York: D. Appleton and Co., 1918. The Mississippi Valley Historical Review, 5 (Mar. 1919): 480-82.

In this book review, Woodson commends the author for the amount of previously unpublished plantation information included, but chides him for shortcomings: failing to indicate types of slaves, lack of understanding of the mind of the black, and presenting slavery as defensible and the slave as satisfied with his lot. Plantation life as presented was characteristic of only the most enlightened slaveholders.

588. "Emma Frances Grayson Merritt." Opportunity, 8 (1930): 244-45.

Born in 1860, Miss Merritt began teaching in 1876. A graduate of Howard University she continued studying and teaching all her life, rising steadily in her profession. Innovative of method, her work became so well known in the District of Columbia that she was called on repeatedly by other school systems. This article was written to honor her retirement.

589. "Emma Frances Grayson Merritt." Southern Workman, 59 (Sept. 1930): 420-22.

Annotation under "Emma Frances Grayson Merritt." Opportunity. See no. 588.

590. "15 Outstanding Events in Negro History." Ebony, 5 (Feb. 1950): 42-46.

The events chosen by Woodson are: Landing of first Negroes; Slaying of Crispus Attucks in Boston Massacre; Heroism of Peter Salem at Bunker Hill; Passing of Ordinance of 1787; Passage of Missouri Compromise; Nat Turner's insurrection; Growth of Abolitionist movement; Launching of Underground Railroad; Compromise of 1850; Dred Scott Decision; Civil War; Reconstruction era; The First Exodus; The Booker T. Washington era; The Great Migration.

591. "A Health Venture with Negro Management." Southern Workman, 60 (1931): 518-24.

Dr. Barnett, a cousin of Woodson's, educated at the University of Michigan and at Howard University, established the Barnett Hospital for blacks in Huntington, W. Va. He persuaded the state to establish a psychiatric hospital for blacks, Lakin Hospital. Urged by the Governor, he relinquished Barnett Hospital to the City and assumed direction of the Lakin Hospital.

592. "Journalism in Schools." Howard University Record, 14 (May 1920): 365-66.

Journalism, though practical, requires a broad cultural background and must deal with people where and as they are and carry them forward. A school of journalism must have a laboratory properly equipped so that during their school careers students can develop in fields suitable for publication.

593. "The Miseducation of the Negro." Crisis, 38 (Aug. 1931): 266-67.

Though Woodson contends that higher education makes misfits of blacks, he does not advocate separate schools nor recommend keeping blacks out of school. He emphasizes the need for teachers who understand the psychology of blacks and are in sympathy with their students, and the reconstruction of curricula to point out the contribution of blacks to culture and civilization.

594. Negro Labor in the United States, 1850-1925, by Charles H. Wesley Ph.D., professor of History in Howard Univer. New York: Vanguard Press, 1927. American Historical Review, 33 (1927): 154-56.

Woodson characterizes Wesley's book as the only scientific treatment of Negro labor in the U.S. It surveys the antebellum condition of slave and free blacks, their capacity for skilled labor, slavery and industrialism, and black labor in the Civil War. The larger part of the book deals with labor in freedom and the struggle for economic rights.

595. "Some Things Negroes Need to Do." <u>Southern Workman</u>, 51 (Jan. 1922): 33-36.

Woodson presented this talk at Hampton Institute, Nov. 5, 1921. He requires five things of blacks: economic independence, educational independence, an independent press, the development of black literature, and the preservation of black records.

Separate Flyer

596. "The Inconsistency of the Negro Radicals." ASNLH, July 29, 1931. 1 page.

Foreign radicals are attempting to induce blacks to join the revolution for an impossible Utopia and to destroy the economic structure in order to correct social wrongs. Such Utopian dreams have never succeeded. Blacks should be radical but in their own interests in order to accumulate sufficient wealth to rise above drudgery and use their talents to advantage.

597. Aery, William Anthony. "Negro Life and History." Southern Workman 60 (1931): 79-81.

This account of the ASNLH Convention in Cleveland enunciates the Association's objectives and tells of Woodson's work as director by summarizing his report. His books are mentioned and his lecture at the opening session on "The Negro in History Rather than Negro History." Also mentioned are the subjects of other lectures.

598. Alexander, Raymond Pace. "The History of the Philadelphia Chapter of the Association for the Study of Negro Life and History." Souvenir Journal 59th Anniversary Meeting of ASNLH. Philadelphia, Pa.: 1974, 20-22.

Judge Alexander's account of the establishing of the Philadelphia Chapter consists largely of a laudatory tribute to Woodson with interesting sidelights on their personal relationship. Describing Woodson and mentioning his warmth and simplicity, he calls him the most renowned and respected black historian in the world.

599. Behling, Agnes. "The Father of Negro History." Negro Digest 12 (Nov. 1962): 6-9.

At the height of what seemed a most successful educational career, Woodson resigned his position to devote the rest of his life to help put blacks back into the history books. A biographical account.

600. Bennett, Lerone, Jr. "Chronicles of Black Courage. Father of Black History Changed Vision of Black America." Ebony 38 (Feb. 1983): 31, 33-34.

A brief biography of Dr. Woodson in which Bennett

lauds him as providing one of the greatest examples in our history of the power of an impassioned individual and emphasizes Woodson's special interest in children and young people.

601. Bennett, Lerone, Jr. "Reading, Riting and Racism." Ebony 22 (March 1967): 130-38.

Racism permeated public school curricula through textbooks which misrepresented or ignored black people, and adversely affected the reading ability of black children. Sensitivity to imbalanced textbooks was aroused by Woodson and ASNLH, W.E.B. DuBois, and others, leading to the Congressional hearing (1966) on "Books for Schools and the Treatment of Minorities."

602. "Black History." (Editorial) Crisis 82 (April 1975): 113-14.

The article states that for many years Woodson's was the only voice of any consequence in Negro historiography, stresses the much greater current interest in Negro history than fifty years ago, and asks if integration will make Negro History Week obsolete. Woodson wished not separateness but that all minorities be integrated into American history.

603. "Carter G. Woodson stamp to be issued in honor of father of black history." Jet 65(Jan. 23, 1984): 22.

604. "Carter Godwin Woodson, 1875-1950." American Sociological Review 15 (June 1950): 441.

A summary of Woodson's life, works and awards, which does not mention, however, his four years in the Philippines.

605. Cox, Pearl Beldon. "People You Know and Love--Men in the Kitchen." Pulse 4 (July 1946): 24-25.

After a brief biography of "our foremost" historian which mentions his fame as a wit and the ladies who haven't been able to "halter him for the altar," there follows a recipe for Woodson's special candy made from brown sugar and black walnuts.

606. DuBois, W.E.B. "Editorial: The Journal of Negro History." Crisis 13 (Dec. 1916): 61.

A handsome tribute to Dr. Woodson and his associates on the completion with the October 1916 number, of the first volume of The Journal of Negro History. DuBois has carefully analyzed the volume and specifies the number of pages devoted to each type of article included.

607. DuBois, W.E.B. "Opinion. History." <u>Crisis</u> 18 (May 1919): 11.

DuBois, realizing the imperative to establish in history the place of American black troops in W.W.I, projected a three-volume history of the war, and sought unsuccessfully to associate with him a board of three or four editors. Dr. Woodson, one of those invited, refused to cooperate except as editor-in-chief.

608. DuBois, W.E.B. "A Portrait of Carter G. Woodson." <u>Masses and Mainstream</u> 3 (June 1950): 19-26.

Contains several errors of fact: that Woodson was 71 at the time of his death, when in fact he was 74; that he was Dean four years at West Virginia State College when he was there two years; that Woodson was 44 in 1922 when he gave up teaching, when he was 46. Since DuBois could not manipulate Woodson any more than anyone else, some of his damning with faint praise in this article may be interpreted in the light of his frustration and these errors.

609. DuBois, W.E.B. "Postscript: The Negro Encyclopedia." <u>Crisis</u> 39 (Aug. 1932): 267-68.

At the first meeting called by the trustees of the Phelps-Stokes Fund to consider the feasibility of publishing a Negro encyclopedia, Nov. 7, 1931, neither DuBois, Alain Locke, nor Dr. Woodson was invited. DuBois and Locke attended the second and third meetings (Jan. 9 and Mar. 12, 1932), but Woodson rejected all persuasion to participate.

610. DuBois, W.E.B. "The White Folk Have a Right to Be Ashamed." <u>The National Guardian</u> 17 (Feb. 7, 1949): 6-7.

A tribute to Woodson who through Negro History Week made the U.S., at least once a year, notice the Negro. The celebration has made millions of white people familiar with a history they would rather forget. Some rich foundation should give Woodson funds to pursue his career without poverty and pain.

611. "The 15 Outstanding Events in Negro History." <u>Ebony</u> 5 (Feb. 1950): 42-43, 47.

The introduction to the article characterizes Woodson as a proud, independent, meticulous pioneer who saw Negro History Week grow to a nationwide event. A biographical account following the article says that success has proven the merit of his idea--to teach America the glories of the Negro's past. Includes the statement that Woodson attended Lincoln (Pa.) University.

612. Fontaine, William T. "'Social Determination' in the Writings of Negro Scholars." <u>American Journal of Sociology</u> 49 (Jan. 1944): 302-313.

By social determination Fontaine means that a correlation exists between the knowledge propounded and the social situations confronting the group, amounting to functional dependence; not, however, mechanical cause-effect sequence. He considers Woodson an example of this, along with E. Franklin Frazier, W.M. Cobb, C.H. Wesley and three others.

613. "Guardian of the Torch of Black History." <u>Ebony</u> 35 (Feb. 1980): 94-98.

Woodson is identified with February because he established Negro History Week celebrated in February, now during the entire month, promoted by Woodson's organization, ASALH. The writer says that Woodson advanced the cause of blacks as much as Martin Luther King, Jr. The article is a picture story of the ASALH.

614. Holmes, John Haynes. "On Presenting the Spingarn Medal." <u>Crisis</u> 32 (Sept. 1926): 231-34.

An address delivered by a white Unitarian minister at the presentation of the Spingarn Medal to Dr. Woodson at the Chicago Conference. A full-page picture of Woodson as Spingarn Medalist appears in the August number, p. 177.

615. "The Horizon: Education." <u>Crisis</u> 20 (Sept. 1920): 240.

A brief notation that Dr. Woodson resigned his position as the Dean of the College of Arts and Sciences at Howard University to become Dean of West Virginia Collegiate Institute.

616. Johnson, Tobe. "The Black College as System." <u>Daedalus</u> 1971 (Summer): 798-812.

Johnson discusses Woodson's views of the nonblack presence on campus, and in support gives three quotations from <u>The Mis-education of the Negro</u>.

617. "Just-Imagine Section on the Faculty." <u>Howard University Record</u> 14 (June 1920): 420.

The student editors ask you to imagine Dean Woodson without his sarcasm.

618. Logan, Rayford W. "Phylon Profile VI: Carter G. Woodson." <u>Phylon</u> 6 (4th Quarter, 1945): 315-21.

Woodson organized ASNLH assuming that knowledge would reduce the emotional area in which prejudice thrives.

Logan quotes laudatory opinions from JNH by outstanding historians and praises the Associated Publishers, whose books are in such demand it cannot be met. He stresses also Woodson's other achievements, his warm human characteristics, and les defauts de ses vertus.

619. Meier, August and Elliott Rudwick. "J. Franklin Jameson, Carter G. Woodson, and the Foundations of Black Historiography." The American Historical Review, 89 (Oct. 1984): 1005-1015.

Jameson played a key role in Woodson's establishment of Afro-American history as a recognized historical discipline. Director of the Department of Historical Research at the Carnegie Institution of Washington, he had long exhibited an interest in black history and admired Woodson's work. He orchestrated with Woodson the ASNLH's application for Carnegie funds, supported his request, and stood "sponsor for the proper expenditure of funds."

620. "Newest Member of Hall of Fame. Honor Goes to Historian Carter G. Woodson." Ebony (Feb. 1958): 26.

See no. 427.

621. Quarles, Benjamin. "What the Historian Owes the Negro: Emergence of long-obscured facets of black history brings with it the challenge to develop new perspectives on this nation's past." Saturday Review (Sept. 3, 1966): 10-13.

After examining the factors which led to ignoring the black's part in American history, Dr. Quarles states that with Woodson black history made a sharp and sudden transition into prominence, and he praises the objectivity of Woodson's publications.

622. Reddick, L.D. "Carter G. Woodson (1875-1950) An Appreciation." Phylon 11 (1950): 177-79.

A warm account which calls Woodson an engaging raconteur and conversationalist and brings out points not usually mentioned: his world view, sense of humor, scorn of pretentiousness, the twinkle in his eye when he said his work was his only wife, and ominous signs in the final year when, less active, Woodson listened more than he talked.

623. Scally, Sister Anthony. "Pioneer Black Historian." Community (Friendship House, Chicago) 29 (Winter 1970): 6-13.

A biographical account of Woodson showing his missionary devotion to presenting the contributions of his people to the culture of his country.

624. Scruggs, Otey M. "Carter G. Woodson, the Negro History Movement, and Africa." Pan African Journal 7 (Spring 1974): 39-50.

Believing that valid history would destroy the myth of white racial superiority, Woodson presented the traditions of African history, showing that black history did not begin with American slavery. He detested European colonialism in Africa and believed that this economic imperialism would be overthrown by black leaders. He saw African cultural elements in Africa in diaspora.

625. Shepperson, George. "Notes on Negro-American Influences on the Emergence of African Nationalism." Journal of African History 1 (1960): 299-312.

The interest of the ASNLH in Africa and the work of Carter Woodson exerted a strong influence on emerging African nationalism. Responses from African leaders are among Woodson's papers in the Library of Congress. Rayford Logan is quoted as saying that the popularization of the study of the African past owes more to Woodson than to DuBois.
Included in Drimmer, Melvin, ed., Black History, A Reappraisal. See no. 517.

626. "The Spingarn Medalist." [Editorial] Opportunity 4 (July 1926): 207.

This award to Woodson carries formal recognition which is not often so richly merited, for by his researches he provided historical background sufficiently accomplished to impress the severest critics of the race, and to give blacks the historical continuity which inspires pride of ancestry. The Spingarn Medal again demonstrates its value and importance.

627. Stuckey, Sterling. "DuBois, Woodson, and the Spell of Africa." Negro Digest 16 (Feb. 1967): 20-24, 60-73.

Stuckey says that Woodson, more than anyone else, popularized African history through his writings and Negro History Week. Woodson devoted five chapters in The Negro in Our History to African history and art, and wrote the comprehensive African Background Outlined. Woodson and DuBois were in essential agreement concerning African consciousness.

628. "Survey of the American Negro in the Professions." Journal of Negro Education 1 (1932): 450.

A report on Dr. Woodson's survey preliminary to his book, The Negro Professional Man and the Community. An official statement from Woodson is quoted, indicating the nature and extent of the work:

questionnaires and personal interviews regarding medicine, dentistry, pharmacy and law.

629. "Survey of the Month." Opportunity 4 (July 1926): 230.

The Spingarn Medal, awarded annually by the NAACP to an American of African descent for highest achievement, was given to Dr. Woodson. This news report includes the terms of the award, lists Woodson's books, and supplies biographical data. J. Franklin Jameson, director of the Carnegie Institution, Washington, was one of those recommending Woodson for the award.

630. Thompson, Charles H. "Editorial Comment: The Association for the Study of Negro Life and History." Journal of Negro Education 4 (Oct. 1935): 465-67.

Summarizing ASNLH's early years and giving an excerpt from Woodson's report at the tenth Annual Meeting, the editorial credits ASNLH with showing that Negro history is a valid field for scholarship, that the Negro will support a worthwhile organization, and that vision, self-sacrifice, and persistence, as exemplified in Woodson, will be rewarded.

631. "Two Doctors of Philosophy." Crisis (July 1912): 119-20.

Both George E. Haynes and Woodson received Ph.D.'s in the spring of 1912. Crisis chose Haynes from Columbia and Woodson from Harvard "Men of the Month" and gave biographical accounts of both. Woodson's includes testimony from his professors that he did his work with distinction, and puts in correct chronological order some events often confused.

632. Winston, Michael R. "Through the Back Door: Academic Racism and the Negro Scholar in Historical Perspective." Daedalus 1971 (Summer): 678-719.

In this long article written when he was not yet 30, Winston devotes one page of chiefly uncomplimentary comments to Dr. Woodson with no documentation for his evaluations, and remarks that the development of the Association for the Study of Negro Life and History was more significant than his contributions as an historian. Five years later in "Carter Godwin Woodson: Prophet of a Black Tradition" (JNH 60: 459-63, see no. 359) he expresses a very different opinion.

633. Wright, C. Ruth. "Negro Authors Week--An Experiment." Crisis 39 (Apr. 1931): 124.

A week devoted to promoting Negro writers, inaugurated

by Dr. R.R. Wright, AME pastor in Philadelphia, proved to be a great success. Eight prominent authors, invited for the week of Dec. 7, 1930, spoke on successive nights. James Weldon Johnson, Kelly Miller, and W.E.B. DuBois preceded Carter G. Woodson who spoke on Thursday. Friday was poets night. Woodson's books were among the best sellers at the exhibit and sale accompanying the event.

6.
Newspaper Articles

Following are titles for some of the columns and articles by Woodson for selected years in four of the black newspapers which gave him publicity. He wrote also for other papers, often repeating his columns. Titles usually indicate contents, so annotations have been supplied only for certain items. Besides these newspapers, Woodson wrote also for the <u>Baltimore Afro-American</u>, <u>Boston Chronicle</u>, <u>Bee</u> (Washington), <u>New York Amsterdam News</u>, <u>Louisiana Weekly</u>, <u>Norfolk Journal and Guide</u>, and Marcus Garvey's <u>Negro World</u>.

The Chicago Defender

634. April 16, 1932. "The Difficulty of Learning from the Depression."

635. April 23, 1932. "A Symposium on Higher Education."

636. May 14, 1932. "An Educational Institution."

637. May 21, 1932. "Is the Educated Negro a Liability?"

638. May 28, 1932. "Vocational Guidance."

639. June 4, 1932. "And So Miss Bowles Goes the Way of Moorland."

640. June 11, 1932. "Exploitation is Not Education."

641. June 18, 1932. "Too Much Hindsight; Insufficient Foresight."

642. June 25, 1932. "And the Negro Loses His Soul."

   Autobiographical account of the influence of his father.

643. July 2, 1932. "Prophets and Profits of Segregation."

644. July 16, 1932. "History of Segregation Parallels That of the History of Slavery."

645. July 30, 1932. "A Rejoinder to Dr. Tobias."

   Woodson states that he did not attack the YMCA but the policies of the organization; he would like to put the Christian back into it.

646. August 13, 1932. "The Failure to Make the Most of Segregation."

647. August 20, 1932. "Are You a Segregationist?"

648. September 17, 1932. "Service Rather than Leadership."

649. September 30, 1932. "Looking at the Negro from Europe."

650. October 1, 1932. "The Black Man and Europe."

651. October 8, 1932. "Europe 25 Years After."

652. January 27, 1934. "Education with Respect to Races."

653. February 10, 1934. "Some Imperfect Reasoning."

654. March 3, 1934. "That Awful Race Problem."

655. March 10, 1934. "Plain Speaking."

656. March 24, 1934. "The Romance of the Creole."

657. April 7, 1934. "Forgotten Romances of Negro History."

658. April 21, 1934. "Why Some Negroes Advocate Segregation."

659. April 28, 1934. "That Mischievous Advisor on Negro Affairs."

660. August 17, 1935. "Explains Opposition to the Study of Race History."

661. September 7, 1935. "Future Task of Race History is Outlined."

662. December 14, 1935. "We as a Race Agree on Nothing."

663. December 28, 1935. "More Teachers, Texts, Needed for Growth of Race History."

664. February 8, 1936. "Writer Says Moral Code of Africans Higher than Our." "Dr. Woodson Declares That Missionaries of U.S., Europe do Better Elsewhere."

665. March 14, 1936. "What's Wrong with Being a Communist?"

New York Age

666. April 18, 1931. "Negro and African Philosophy and Art Should Have Place in Courses Offered by Race Schools, Colleges. Dr. Carter G. Woodson Declares Greek Philosophy and European Thought Occupy Greater Part of Negro Colleges Curricula."

667. May 30, 1931. "Why 'Highly Educated' Ministers Preach to Benches."

668. June 6, 1931. "The Mis-Education of the Negro in Economics."

> Because whites control production many are drifting to socialism and communism. To overthrow capitalism will take many years and the Negro will be starved out so he must do the so-called impossible.

669. June 13, 1931. "Politics in the Schools."

670. June 20, 1931. "Complete Program Announced for National Negro Business League Session."

671. June 27, 1931. "The Negro Graduates."

672. July 4, 1931. "Negro Trail Blazers a Necessity."

673. July 18, 1931. "Only the Trail Blazer in Business Succeeds."

674. July 25, 1931. "Negroes Look in Vain for Help from Without."

> Religion, education and politics have been held up as panaceas to the Negro, but are not. The Negro must learn to think for himself as an independent, not controlled by others.

675. August 1, 1931. "The Inconsistency of Negro Radicals."

> [Also published as a separate flyer.]

676. August 8, 1931. "The Negro Must Appeal to his Own."

677. August 15, 1931. "A United Negro Church."

678. August 22, 1931. "Opposition to Union of Negro Churches."

679. August 29, 1931. "Difficulties in Way of United Church."

680. September 5, 1931. "Union of Churches Considered Utopian."

681. September 12, 1931. "Radical Proposals With Respect to United Negro Church."

682. September 19, 1931. "Disunion of the Churches Accounts for the Negro Preacher in Politics."

683. September 26, 1931. "Church Edifices Declared to be Property in Mortmain."

Negroes invest unwisely in Church property.

684. October 2, 1931. "Theology a Factor in Disunion of Churches."

685. October 10, 1931. "Superfluous Negro Preachers Prevent the Union of the Churches.'

686. October 17, 1931. "Need for Union Emphasized by Recent Data of the Churches."

687. October 24, 1931. "Negro Church to be Subjected to the Acid Test at Historical Meeting."

688. October 31, 1931. "The Contribution of the West Indian to America: A Topic of the Historical Meeting in New York City."

689. November 7, 1931. "West Indian Racial Purity Considered an Advantage."

690. November 14, 1931. "Woodson as an Iconoclast."

691. November 21, 1931. "Finding the Negro Community and Working in It."

692. November 28, 1931. "The Increasing Desire to Know the Truth."

693. December 5, 1931. "Facts of Church Corruption Called Half-Baked Opinions."

694. December 12, 1931. "The Side-Show of the George Washington Bicentennial."

While there is no objection to showing Negroes as George Washington's slaves, the place of free patriots, such as Crispus Attucks, Benjamin Banneker, and such a writer as Phillis Wheatley should also be presented.

695. December 19, 1931. "Traducing the Negro to Honor George Washington."

696. December 26, 1931. "Eliminating the Negro from the George Washington Bicentennial."

Traducers planning the Bicentennial called in three genuflecting Negroes and proposed separate celebration for the Negro.

697. January 2, 1932. "The George Washington Bicentennial Eliminates March 5, Crispus Attucks Day."

698. January 9, 1932. "The 18th Century Negro More Courageous than the Negro of the 20th."

699. January 16, 1932. "George Washington as He Was."

700. January 23, 1932. "Negroes More Outspoken a Century Ago Than Today."

701. January 30, 1932. "Why the Negro Cannot Move Forward."

702. February 6, 1932. "An Appeal for Assistance in the Study of Negro Life and History."

703. February 13, 1932. "The Need for True Dramatization of Negro Life."

704. February 20, 1932. "What the Negro Has to Dramatize."

705. February 27, 1932. "Blessings of the Depression."

706. March 5, 1932. "Impediments to Cooperation Among Negroes."

707. March 12, 1932. "Do We Get What We Deserve?"

708. March 19, 1932. "Youth Trying to Find a Way."

709. March 26, 1932. "The Difficulty of Learning from the Depression."

710. April 2, 1932. "The Poverty of the Depression Not Alarming."

711. April 9, 1932. "The Meager Contribution to Leadership in Washington."

712. April 16, 1932. "How to Get Out of the Bread Line."

713. April 23, 1932. "A Symposium on Higher Education."

714. April 30, 1932 "Do You Study the Negro? Do You Know Him?"

715. May 7, 1932. "Vocational Guidance."

716. May 14, 1932. "An Educational Institution."

Miss Burroughs' school--examples of her successful students.

717. May 21, 1932. "Is the Educated Negro a Liability?"

718. May 28, 1932. "Is the Negro a Business Failure?"

719. June 4, 1932. "And So Miss Bowles Goes the Way of Moorland."

720. June 11, 1932. "Exploitation is Not Education."

721. June 18, 1932. "Too Much 'Hindsight,' Insufficient Foresight."

Woodson explains his resignation from the staff of the DAB.

722. June 25, 1932. "And the Negro Loses His Soul."

An autobiographical account of the influence of his father.

723. July 2, 1932. "Prophets and Profits of Segregation."

724. October 14, 1932. "Sending the Wrong Negro to Europe."

725. October 21, 1932. "Advertising the Race Abroad."

726. October 28, 1932. "Pioneers Wanted Abroad."

Autobiographical reference to offer of a position abroad in 1907.

727. November 4, 1932. "Leave a Javelin at the Door."

Autobiographical reference to meeting the Countess of Jumilhav.

728. November 11, 1932. "Self-Assertion in Africa."

729. November 18, 1932. "A New Step in Negro Education."

730. November 25, 1932. "Purchasing the Badge of Inferiority."

Discusses the Negro inferiority complex which has been instilled by the schools.

731. December 2, 1932. "Last Excuse of the Derelict Removed."

A committee recently appointed by ASNLH will plan and

outline courses in Negro history so there will be no further excuse for dereliction of duty in teaching Negro history in the schools.

732. December 9, 1932. "First Scientific Study of Negro in the Professions."

A review of the book, <u>The Negro Professional Man and the Community</u>.

733. December 16, 1932. "Negro History Week Again."

734. December 30, 1933. "Holding the Negro Between Him and the Fire."

Autobiographical reference to meeting Booker T. Washington, and to threats of lynching.

735. January 6, 1934. "How to Get From Between the Other Fellow and the Fire."

736. January 13, 1934. "Teaching Negroes Deliberately and Specifically."

737. January 20, 1934. "Sounding a New Note for Negro History Week."

738. January 27, 1934. "Differentiation in Education with Respect to Races."

739. February 3, 1934. "Negro History Week--Feb. 11-18."

740. February 10, 1934. "Distinguish Between Significant and Insignificant."

741. February 17, 1934. "Varying Conceptions of History."

742. February 24, 1934. "Forgotten Negroes."

743. March 3, 1934. "That Awful Race Problem."

744. March 10, 1934. "History Lost by Emphasizing Trifles."

745. March 17, 1934. "Forgotten Romance of Negro History."

Woodson tells the story of Estevanico, of Cudjoe and the Maroons of Jamaica and of the city of Palmares in Pernambuco.

746. March 24, 1934. "The Romance of the Creole."

Madison Washington's life was dominated by his desire for freedom and his love for his wife. He ventured to free her from slavery. Seized and put aboard a ship bound for New Orleans, he organized a mutiny.

747. March 31, 1934.   "The Hero of Amistad."

Cinque gave the world a new idea of the African's love of freedom by his revolt on the "Amistad."

748. April 7, 1934.   "Truth in the Battle with Error."

749. April 14, 1934.   "That Mischievous Advisor on Negro Affairs."

750. April 21, 1934.   "Why Some Negroes Advocate Segregation."

751. February 23, 1935.   "Woodson Misquoted on the Church."

752. March 30, 1935.   "Negro History Association Reaches Another Landmark."

753. April 6, 1935.   "Negro History Association Seeks $30,000 Fund."

754. August 3, 1935.   "What the Association for the Study of Negro Life and History Celebrates this Year."

755. August 10, 1935.   "The $30,000 Campaign of the ASNLH."

756. August 17, 1935.   "Opposition to Negro History Explained."

757. August 24, 1935.   "Program for the Celebration of the 20th Anniversary of History Assoc. [sic] in Chicago."

758. August 31, 1935.   "Historical Association in the Celebration of its 20th Anniversary Faces the Future."

759. September 7, 1935.   "The African Situation to be Discussed at Negro History Association's Celebration."

760. September 21, 1935.   "Association for the Study of Negro Life and History Celebrates 20th Anniversary."

761. November 16, 1935.   "New Treatment of Richard Allen's Life in Biography Written by Charles H. Wesley."

762. November 30, 1935.   "Negro History Week Literature Distributed Free of Charge."

763. December 7, 1935.   "Increased Interest Noted in the Dramatization of the Negro."

In earlier times abroad the Negro figured prominently in drama; e.g., Othello and plays of Lope de Vega.

764. December 14, 1935.   "What Aspect of Negro Life and History Would You Dramatize?"

Willis Richardson included two plays on Africa in
Negro History in 13 Plays.

765. December 21, 1935. "Abyssinia in Negro History Week."

766. January 4, 1936. "Why the Negro Lacks his Tenth."

During Negro History Week concentrate on actual
achievements, not overestimating the insignificant or
eulogizing the unimportant. Most foreigners think
that because the Negro is 1/10 of the population he
has 1/10 of everything else: wealth, offices in
government, etc.

767. January 11, 1936. "Accumulating with $100 a Month."

768. January 18, 1936. "How the African Surpasses His
Traducers."

769. January 25, 1936. "The Higher Standard of Living."

770. February 1, 1936. "History and Not Eulogy."

771. February 8, 1936. "The Month for Celebrations."

772. February 15, 1936. "Negro History Week in its Proper
Setting."

773. February 22, 1936. "Keeping the Record."

774. February 29, 1936. "George Washington."

775. March 7, 1936. "The Next Oath."

776. March 14, 1936. "Why Call the Negro Red?"

Autobiographical reference to communism.

777. March 21, 1936. "Emancipation of the Negro Voter."

778. March 28, 1936. "What Negro Do You Hate?"

779. April 4, 1936. "The Loyalty of the Negro Questioned
Again."

In crises such as our several wars, the Negro has
always proved loyal.

About Woodson in New York Age

780. January 24, 1931. "College and High School Education
Makes Majority of Negroes without Value in the Uplift of
their Race. Dr. Carter Woodson, Director Negro History
Study, Declares the Longer Negroes Attend School the Worse
Off They Are."

781. June 13, 1931. "'Interracial Cooperation in Business' to be Theme of Annual Session of Negro Business League. [June 21-24.]"

782. June 27, 1931. "National Business League Now in Session in New York City."

783. November 14, 1931. "Negro History Association Holds Successful Meeting in New York."

784. June 18, 1932. "Tobias Replies to Woodson's Attack on Y.M.C.A."

> Excluding members of either race group from other units shows how far the Y. still has to go. Negro leadership does not believe that because the Y. is unable to achieve all ideals at once they should sever all connections with whites as associates. Regret Dr. Woodson should declare he will never again contribute. Dr. Tobias says, "Personally I hope he will repent of his repentence because I believe thoroughly in the fine work to which he has devoted his life."

785. June 25, 1932. "Woodson Replies to Article by Dr. Tobias."

> Dr. Woodson replies that he did not attack the Y. as an institution, but questioned the Christianity of those who claim to be carrying out its policies.

786. December 23, 1932. "Committee on What We Should Teach the Negro About Himself and About Others in Relation to Himself, Makes Report."

Pittsburgh Courier

787. September 3, 1932. "Independent Thinking and Voting is Needed."

788. December 3, 1932. "If I were Living in Atlanta."

789. December 17, 1932. "Women Should Have More Voice in Our Affairs--Woodson."

790. December 24, 1932. "Columbia Professor Strikes a New Note in Negro Education."

About Woodson in Pittsburgh Courier

791. August 13, 1932. "Most of Us are Segregationists."

Washington Tribune

792. May 3, 1924. "College Women Convene Here."

793. December 13, 1924. "Omega Psi Phi Fraternity to Hold Annual Conclave Here."

794. December 27-31, 1924. "Among the Prominent Omega Men Who Will be Honored at this Smoker is Dr. Carter G. Woodson."

795. September 5, 1925. "Association for the Study of Negro Life and History to Meet Here Next Week."

796. September 12, 1925. "Important Items Discussed by Historical Body."

797. November 7, 1925. "New Works on Our Bookshelf."

Review of <u>Negro Orators and Their Orations</u>.

798. November 25, 1925. "Carter G. Woodson Refuses to be Speaker with President Durkee of Howard."

7.
Dissertations and Theses

799. Woodson, Carter G. "The Disruption of Virginia." Unpublished Ph.D. Diss., Harvard Univ., 1912.

This is not available at the Library of Congress, but there is a microfilm copy of a TS in the West Virginia University Library, Morgantown, W. Va.

800. Fullinwider, Samuel. "The Negro Mind, 1890-1930." Unpublished Ph.D. Diss., Univ. of Wisconsin, 1967.

A well-written study, it makes a significant contribution to the understanding of black intellectual thought from the Era of Booker T. Washington through the Harlem Renaissance. [Contributed by Dr. J.A. Goggin.]

801. Goggin, Jacqueline A. "Carter G. Woodson and the Movement to Promote Black History." Unpublished Ph.D. Diss., Univ. of Rochester, 1983.

Woodson pioneered the institutionalized inquiry into black history through the ASNLH. He stimulated a generation of younger black scholars, showed race as a factor in international and domestic relations, stressed African culture, combatted racist historiography and pointed out the flaws in the educational system which led to the "mis-education" of blacks.

802. Grimes, Joseph A. "A Study of Negro Historians, 1844-1920." Unpublished M.A. Thesis, Univ. of Iowa, 1935.

This is a creatively constructed though rather awkwardly written outline of early black historiography; it provided the groundwork for Earl E. Thorpe's Negro Historians in the United States. [contributed by Dr. J.A. Goggin.]

803. Hale, Noreen. "Carter Godwin Woodson: Historian of the Negro American." Unpublished M.A. Thesis, Univ. of San Francisco, 1969.

Elucidates Woodson's contribution to American historiography by analysis of his works.

804. Harris, Janette Hoston. "Charles Harris Wesley, Educator and Historian: 1891-1947." Unpublished Ph.D. Diss., Howard Univ., 1975.

Decribes Wesley's close connection with Woodson and his definitive part in ASNLH.

805. Romero, Patricia Watkins. "Carter G. Woodson: A Biography." Unpublished Ph.D. Diss., Ohio State Univ., 1971.

A comprehensive evaluative chronological biography.

806. Thomas, Richard A. "Carter G. Woodson: A Critical Study of His Contribution to Black Historiography." Unpublished M.S. Thesis, Michigan State Univ., 1971.

807. Yates, Ella Gaines. "An Annotated Cumulative Index to the Journal of Negro History." Unpublished M.A. Thesis, Atlanta Univ., 1951.

Covers the period 1916-1940. Facilitates research dealing with articles written by Woodson and also the general thrust of material in the JNH during that period. Also helpful in providing a brief historical sketch of ASNLH. [Contributed by Dr. J.A. Goggin.]

808. Young, Alfred. "The Educational Philosophies of Booker T. Washington and Carter G. Woodson: A Liberating Praxis." Unpublished Ph.D. Diss., Syracuse Univ., 1977.

Based upon the assumptions of Paulo Freire, the study suggests that the educational philosophies of Booker T. Washington and Carter G. Woodson were primarily concerned with the liberation of black Americans.

Appendix: Notes on Manuscript Collections

Notes on Manuscript Collections

Numbers in brackets refer to relevant items in the bibliography.

One would expect to find the major portion of Woodson's papers at the Carter G. Woodson Center in Washington, D.C., the headquarters of the Association for the Study of Afro-American Life and History, but would be disappointed to find but little help there in this regard at this time. More profitable would be the documents in the Carter G. Woodson Collection of Negro Papers and Related Documents in the Manuscript Division of the Library of Congress which Woodson deposited from 1920-1938 [553]. Dated 1803-1936, the bulk of the material falls into the period 1830-1927, and includes diaries, addresses, legal documents and clippings, which Woodson collected and deposited in the Library of Congress for safekeeping. Letters to him are from prominent men and women such as John E. Bruce, George Washington Carver, Booker T. Washington, John R. Lynch, Zora Neale Hurston, Mrs. Booker T. Washington, the historian Edward Channing, and several African correspondents. Some other persons, not as well known, wrote Woodson very interesting letters which have also been preserved in this collection [451]. In the Abel Doysié papers in the Library of Congress are two letters written by Woodson in Paris (1933) and a reply. The J. Franklin Jameson Papers in the Library of Congress also contain Woodson letters.

Equally as useful are the papers preserved in the Manuscript Division of the Moorland Spingarn Research Center at Howard University, Washington, D.C. The Jesse E. Moorland papers contain an extensive correspondence between Woodson and Moorland concerning the first few years of the Association for the Study of Negro Life and History when Moorland was Secretary-Treasurer [454]. The Center also contains a small collection of Carter G. Woodson papers, and more letters in other collections, such as the Archibald Grimké papers, the Francis Grimké papers, and the Angelina Grimké papers. Significant items are in the Benjamin G. Brawley Collection papers and the Kelly Miller papers, and a small number in the J. Stanley Durkee papers, as well as a few other collections.

The National Archives provides complete documentation on Woodson's appointment to the Philippine Islands and the exchange of letters between Woodson and the War Department (Record Group 350. Bureau of Insular Affairs).* Two letters, one from Robert Woodson and one from Bessie Woodson to the Department of Insular Affairs express the wish of the entire Woodson family to move to the Philippine Islands to be with Carter Woodson [453].

Useful in the controversy between Carter Woodson and Thomas Jesse Jones [44] is a document in the Anson Phelps Stokes papers, Yale University Library: "Phelps-Stokes Confidential Memorandum for the Trustees of the Phelps-Stokes Fund regarding Dr. Carter G. Woodson's attacks on Dr. Thomas Jesse Jones," dated May 22, 1924. Included in this document is the letter sent to Dr. Woodson by the editors of The Freeman asking for a statement regarding his differences with Dr. Jones, March 13, 1924, and Woodson's reply published in The Freeman, which gave rise to Anson Phelps Stokes' "Memorandum" in defense of Jones. The Yale University Library also contains the James Weldon Johnson papers which include some correspondence of Carter G. Woodson.

The National Union Catalogue of Manuscript Collections lists the Montgomery Bell papers (Nannie Seawell Boyd collection), Tennessee State Library and Archives, and the Schomburg Papers at the Schomburg Center for Research in Black Culture, New York Public Library, as including correspondence with Carter G. Woodson. The Laura Spelman Rockefeller Memorial, Records, in the Rockefeller Archive Center, Pocanto Hills, N.Y., contains some correspondence with Carter G. Woodson, as well as material relating to the Association for the Study of Negro Life and History. The Woodson papers in the General Education Board collection are located here also. In the Archives of the Carnegie Corporation of New York, in New York City, are materials related to the Association and to Carter Woodson.

The Washington Post (2/24/85) reported that a large collection of letters and documents of Carl Murphy, editor and publisher of the Afro-American Newspapers, 1922-1967, arrived at the Moorland-Spingarn Research Center, Howard University. The deposit, as yet uncataloged, contains correspondence with Carter G. Woodson.

---

* Newman, Debra. Black History, A Guide to Civilian Records in the National Archives. Washington, D.C., National Archives Trust Fund Board, General Services Administration, 1984. p. 330-31.

Manuscript Collections

Where indicated the listing is from the <u>National Union Catalogue of Manuscript Collections</u>. The numbers to the right of these entries refer to the reference numbers in the <u>National Union Catalogue of Manuscript Collections</u>.

Carter G. Woodson file.
Jessie E. Moorland file.
Moorland Spingarn Research Center, Archives.
Howard University.

Francis J. Grimké (1830-1937) papers.   62-4112
Howard University
Includes letters relating to Grimke's will from C.G. Woodson

Montgomery Bell papers (Nannie Seawell Boyd, coll.) 64-1175
Tennesses State Library and Archives.
(Bell established iron furnaces in Tenn.)
Correspondents include C.G. Woodson.

Abel Doysié (1886) papers.   68-2020
Library of Congress, MS Division
Employed as representative in Paris of the Carnegie Institution of Washington, D.C., Doysié was researcher, historian, translator. Correspondence includes two letters written by Woodson in Paris, and a reply.

Carter Godwin Woodson collection.   68-2089
Library of Congress, MS Division.
The papers consist primarily of correspondence on a number of subjects including Negro history. Dated 1803-1936, but bulk of material falls in period 1830-1927.

Laura Spelman Rockefeller Memorial. Records. 74-960
Rockefeller Foundation Archives, New York City.
Correspondence, minutes and dockets, etc., chiefly before 1930. Organizations include ASNLH. Correspondents include Carter G. Woodson.

James Weldon Johnson papers.   74-1211
Yale University Library.
Correspondents include Carter G. Woodson.

National Archives, Washington, D.C. Record Group 8898.
"Records of the Department of War, Bureau of Insular Affairs."
All the correspondence concerning Woodson's appointment to the Philippine Islands.

Schomburg (1874-1938) papers.   79-1890
New York Public Library. Schomburg Center for Research in Black Culture.
Includes correspondence with Carter G. Woodson.

Certificate of Incorporation, ASNLH, recorded Oct. 2, 1915, at 10:49 a.m. in Liber 31 at Folio 441 as Instrument #13939, Office of the Recorder of Deeds, Washington, D.C.

Carter G. Woodson correspondence
Robert Moton Papers
Tuskegee Institute.
Carnegie Library Archives.

Robert Clifton Weaver, papers.
U.S. Secretary, H.U.D.
New York Public Library, Schomburg Center for Research in Black Culture.
Includes correspondence with Carter G. Woodson.

Anson Phelps Stokes "Confidential Memorandum for the Trustees of the Phelps-Stokes Fund regarding Dr. Carter G. Woodson's attacks on Dr. Thomas Jesse Jones."
Yale University Library.

Index

A